I'M OK,
You're
NOT OK

*Experiences of Having a Loved One With a
Personality Disorder*

D0954369

BY

LINDA S. BUDD, PHD

ISBN: 1481185896

ISBN 13:   9781481185899

Library of Congress Control Number: 2012923312
CreateSpace Independent Publishing Platform
North Charleston, SC

Acknowledgements

No book is written without help, particularly if I am the author. First, I would like to thank all the families who have shared their stories. Without them I could not have begun to understand the pain the family often experiences behind closed doors. Obviously, I cannot mention them by name, but I am sure they will recognize their parts in the stories told here.

Next, I would like to thank my team of first-line editors. My friend and fellow therapist, Dr. Tamara Kaiser has spent unending hours challenging and assisting me both in my writing and in my clinical work. Then there is my friend, Kathy McClure, who served not only as an editor, but non-therapist reader. It is she who came up with the title of the book. Finally, Heather Tibbles-Vassilev, who carpools with my husband, offers editing from a scientific and technical vantage point.

This work began with the professional literary advice of Scott Edelstein, who has always answered my publishing questions. Patti Frazee helped tune my words to make my points become clearer. Thank you to both of them.

Finally, I would like to thank my husband, Jeffrey Budd. Without his patience, his willingness to ask me what I meant by certain words, and his computer savvy, this work would never have come into fruition. Thank you for your wisdom and support.

Introduction:

INTRODUCTION:

How Does This Feel?

Is there someone in your life who saps your strength? Someone who seems to take more and more of your energy and yet leaves you feeling it is never enough. This person may be your sister, your brother, your mother, your father, your wife, your husband, your dating partner, your adult child...

It's as if you can't do anything right for this person. No matter how hard you try, this person gets angry, sad, sick, and gives you the message that it's all *your* fault. In fact, he truly believes he is fine, and the problems he experiences are the result of other people's mistakes, choices, inadequacies, or wrongdoing.

This person may walk into a room and need to be the center of attention. He attempts to train family members to keep him in the center. If not, he whines, sulks, is openly angry or falls into a silent rage and makes the rest of the family suffer. If you don't do what he wants, he feels rejected or punished.

This person works hard to get other people or family members to see how she has been hurt and betrayed by you when all you do is try to fulfill what she says she needs. This person constantly tries to control your behavior instead of her own. In this person's reality *you* are the bad one, and she has done nothing wrong. She is *your* victim. She has no idea of how she perpetrates the people who love her the most.

This person can be charming and delightful to you, especially when others are around; and then change in the blink of an eye and rant at you alone. What happened? What did you do wrong? You find yourself "walking on eggshells." You find yourself doing anything to keep the peace, but each day you are a little more tired. Each day you grow less and less your-self. You feel both guilty, because she says you are the problem, and crazy, because you know you are not the one yelling and acting out. She may even try to convince you that you are wrong and too rigid for believing you have to obey the laws.

Over the course of my thirty-five years of practice as a psychologist, I have become intrigued with what a person with borderline or antisocial personality disorder looks like. There is a body of information that is not well known outside the mental health field. It is the knowledge we have about personality disorders.

People who have certain personality disorders seem like vampires to some family members. It feels as if having a relationship with this person mandates that you offer up your very blood—your essence of life—to main-tain the relationship. However, in the end that is not enough. The thirst is unquenchable. This illness has led those with personality disorder to develop blood-sucking coping skills because they believe they need the skills in order to survive. Little do they know that this coping mechanism helps to create their own misery.

The person with personality disorder functions always out of a Self Only Survival (SOS) mode. They are not aware that their survival modality causes the person they love a sense of being angry, traumatized, and confused, and may yield debt, destruction, death, and abandonment.

Parents naturally feel protective and compassionate. Setting bound-aries with an adult child with SOS, which in her world means you're not agreeing with her, is an especially difficult thing to do. As a parent, you become confused. Is it really okay to disobey laws, like driving without a license? If you get her through just one more trauma will she learn to function on her own? You may have spent your life believing *if I can just love her enough or take care of her enough, she will be whole.* You have the belief that love heals all.

However, because the problem lies *within* your loved one, no amount of your love or work will fix it. Ultimately, the SOS person will simply redefine the situation. Because she is terrified of abandonment or loss of control, she continually sets herself up to be abandoned or to lose control. In her mind she will begin to believe you don't love her. She will sense your frustration and exasperation with her neediness either to be taken care of or be in control and conclude that "you don't love me." She is the master of the double bind—a situation in which you are wrong if you do what she asks and you are wrong if you don't do what she asks. For instance, if she needs money and you loan it to her, she will pay you back when she sees fit, if at all, and may never even say thank you for the loan. If you ask for a payment or a schedule of payment, you are bad for thinking she is incompetent or irresponsible with money, or you are simply cheap and too rigid about money. The fact that you loved her enough to try to help does not register in her mind. You are now the problem.

SOS people often have different realities from the people with whom they live and upon whom they depend. They cannot absorb how they create their own problems so they develop realities about how others are mean to them, mistreat them, victimize them. Their thinking is concrete. You are either for them or against them. Against them often simply means you don't give them what they want or buy into their reality.

Your loved one lacks the ability to think from another person's perspective. There is only one reality—theirs. An example would be the woman who keeps five other people waiting for thirty minutes while she brushes her hair. An apology is simply out of the question for *she* is the victim, not the five people waiting. You were rude when you asked her to hurry.

The person with borderline or antisocial personality disorder has a mental illness. They do not set out to victimize the people around them even though this behavior is consistent over time. They are completely unable to comprehend their impact upon others.

Why does personality disorder develop? Are people born with it? Can parents, siblings, spouses make it worse or better? It is important to recognize whether you are living with or related to someone who has a personality disorder and who functions in that self only survival (SOS) mode. In the following chapters, I will discuss why and how personality disorder may develop or if the person is born with it. I will describe characteristics and games those with personality disorder unknowingly play for what they believe is their own survival. All of this will be in the context of the interpersonal relationships as a parent, sibling, spouse or child of a loved one with a personality disorder. I will recount stories that have been related to me in my office. All stories are altered, and some are combinations of two or more families to protect the families' privacy.

I am a psychologist and marriage and family therapist. I am best known for my work with children—children who have challenging temperaments. I am the author of two books: *Living With the Active Alert Child* and *The Journey of Parenting: Helping Your Child Become A Competent, Caring, Contributing Adult*. In my work with children with challenging temperaments I have attracted to my caseload many people whose children had issues other than being overly active and alert. Sometimes the children brought to me really had other problems such as Tourette's Syndrome, bipolar disorder, divorcing parents or parents who had a personality disorder. If their parents didn't have a personality disorder, they often had an aunt, an uncle, a grandparent who seemed to fit a personality disorder profile.

We do not know why personality disorder develops. As Marsha Linehan, a specialist in treating personality disorders frequently states, "People with personality disorders are born with more challenging temperaments."

My focus in this book is not on children because I don't believe children are born with personality disorders. I do, however, believe in temperament. Children are different from each other at birth. Some children are more challenging, beginning from birth. The personality disorder develops when the child's sensitivity is not moderated in the environment in which the child grows up.

People with personality disorder often have a history in childhood of actual abuse or neglect. Many professionals believe this is the only way that personality disorders develop. However, from my experience, I believe overly sensitive children can see many experiences in life as abuse or neglect even when it is not intended to be. I have known families in which children, both biological and adopted, have developed the personality disorder over time. The family had no history of abuse or neglect. Certainly in the case of the adopted children it was not always clear what the first few weeks or months of the child's life had been like—was he abused or neglected in the foster home before the adoptive parents got him? In the case of biological children, the parents were unaware of any abuse or neglect with a babysitter or daycare, but they felt fairly confident it had not occurred.

I have also worked with parents of adult children who did not believe their child had a challenging temperament as a child. Instead, the parent described the child as too eager to please.

We simply do not know why personality disorders develop. It seems to be some combination of genetics, biochemistry, and environment. Some studies about borderline personality disorder find that the disorder is 50 to 60 percent inheritable.

By the time a professional sees a young adult and is willing to use a personality disorder diagnosis there may often have been an incident or an environment the young adult calls abusive or neglectful. In many cases there actually was abuse or neglect, i.e., the young adult had been raped or had a parent who ignored their needs.

What fascinates me is the difference between the person who was raped or abused and works hard to be a survivor (i.e., does not have a personality disorder) and the person who constantly sees any incident as abuse and forever takes a victim stance. From that victim stance they use their history to manipulate others to take care of them, to not be responsible, to never develop into a mature adult—they are a victim and everyone else is to take care of them (do their bidding), because such and such happened to them.

When the person is twenty to thirty years past the trauma, they still use the same rationale: bad things happened to me so I don't have to be responsible. They seem to collect a litany of bad things, such as divorces, job problems, health issues, debt, deaths of people or pets, etc., which in their mind provide justification for their behavior.

Curiously, it never enters their mind that bad things happen to all of us. They work at making sure their list is longer than anyone else's, whether real or not. Their list is worse than yours, and therefore they are in need of more sympathy from the world.

With an antisocial personality disorder the person breaks laws, lies, and justifies their behavior with the belief they deserve what they are getting because they are the victim of our society, its laws, greed by big business, greed from an ex-spouse—everybody else does it. A person with an antisocial disorder acts as if he is more "special" than the rest of us, and therefore the laws of society or needs of community do not apply to him. Many people, when they hear the word antisocial, think of the word psychopath.

They think of people like Charlie Manson and Jeffrey Dahmer (horrific mass murderers) or, more recently, Bernie Madoff (a financial mass murderer of sorts). The jails are filled with people like this.

However, in this book, I am referring to people with antisocial personality who are repeatedly skirting the laws or rules (i.e. driving without insurance, having affairs, etc.) but may not do so at such a level as to be incarcerated or, if so, only for a brief time. In a way they are simply at a lower level of antisocial personality disorder. This person can be anyone from a CEO to your best friend's husband.

The damage due to borderline or antisocial personality disorders is felt by their families and acquaintances. These behaviors eventually become tiresome to other family members who create distance from their loved one or even abandon them just as they have always feared.

As a family member, if you hang in there, you have to work hard to maintain a sane reality and not buy into their multiple distortions. If you cannot do that, you may discover you are losing yourself, your money, and possibly your connections to healthier people as they lead you through their strange, dark world. Remember the vampire analogy. Vampires in the old stories did not wish to feed upon those they loved. They did it for survival, knowing no other way to survive. They became good at it and eventually fearful of daylight (truth) and the world. They knew of no other way to function. They were terrified that without their SOS behaviors they would not survive.

In the coming chapters there will be many examples of this dynamic. All the stories are true. Some are a combination of stories from multiple families. The names and identifying characteristics have been changed to protect the true identities of the families involved. In reading these stories it is my hope that families will be able to identify themselves and choose different paths than the families I have portrayed in the stories. If any pain can be averted, I will be gratified.

RECOGNITION

CHAPTER ONE:

Recognition and Professionals

A. How to Recognize a Personality Disorder

There are several pervasive patterns a professional looks for to diagnose a personality disorder.

Let me differentiate borderline personality disorder (BPD) from antisocial personality disorder (ASPD). It is not always true but, historically, professionals presume more women than men are diagnosed with BPD; whereas, many more men than women are diagnosed with ASPD. However, statistically, our studies of people with BPD show roughly the same number of men and women diagnosed with BPD across the larger population in the United States.

Antisocial personality disordered (ASPD) individuals may privately enjoy being able to con or put something over on someone else. There seems to be two ways to display ASPD, as described by Stan Kapuchinski, MD. "Mr. Slick" is quite seductive, like a con man. "Mr. Bully" is more physically or emotionally manipulative and not above using violent or aggressive behavior. An ASPD individual will be involved in illegal behavior and breaking laws; more so than a borderline personality disordered person (BPD). It is as if the ASPD person believes rules do not apply to them. He takes great pleasure in getting away with things.

Either disorder can be experienced similarly by loved ones. The person with ASPD disregards the *laws*, not just the *rules*. People with ASPD will more easily exhibit rages that can escalate to violence or physical abuse.

Although this is possible with a person with BPD, it is more prevalent with ASPD.

People with BPD escalate emotionally to manipulate others, whereas for those with ASPD it is about both physical and emotional control. People with BPD are often very intelligent and consciously or unconsciously get others to do their dirty work. With those who have ASPD other people do their dirty work out of fear for physical safety.

One way to think about the difference between ASPD and BPD is to distinguish the hidden agenda behind the behavior. The person with BPD is desperate to not be abandoned. The one with ASPD wants control and power.

There will be many stories in this book about people with these disorders. Some you may identify as happening in your life. If you do, ask yourself if this was an isolated incident, or if this was just one instance of a consistent, cumulative narrative that fits this person about whom you are thinking? Some people may have a few traits of a personality disorder or accidentally display some traits but do not have the full-blown disorder. As always, BPDs and ASPDs may be somewhere on the continuum.

The stories in these sections are meant to be brief glimpses into a family's life. Their purpose is to give examples of the patterns that evolve in a family. These stories are to help you, the reader, understand concretely what emotional dysregulation, entitlement, etc., look like within a family. In later chapters I give more detailed descriptions of how the family looks over time.

B. What Professionals Know and Do Not Know

In so many ways life tries to teach us what we cannot control. You do not control the temperament with which your child comes into the world. You do not get to choose or control who you are given as a child, sibling or a parent. You do control with whom you choose to live with as a spouse or partner. Often the choice of a spouse or partner are made early in our lives when we are still only learning about ourselves and other people. Nevertheless, if you are self-aware, you do have the choice of how you exercise control of yourself, not simply reacting to your loved one with BPD or ASPD.

The question then becomes what do I do when related to someone with BPD or ASPD? A client in my office once quoted an unknown source, "Relationships are not chewing gum: to be chewed up and tossed away." Yet the person with the personality disorder seems to follow different rules. They may challenge you to see them as chewing gum to be discarded. As one mother who was afraid to set limits said, "I am so afraid that my daughter will have no one in her future." However, if the mother hangs in there and sets no limits, this reiterates to her daughter what she already believes: "Everyone has to adapt to me, I don't have any responsibility to adapt to others." The daughter does not knowingly set out to act in this manner. She is not aware of how she impacts those around her; she is only aware of how other people impact her.

Throughout this book I will give examples of how a person with either ASPD or BPD affects the people they love the most. My belief is the ASPD or BPD individual does love family members, but because of the illness they are not capable of seeing beyond their own needs, much like a two year old's brain is incapable of viewing life from another's stance or seeing their impact upon another. Both borderline personality disorder and anti-social personality disorder people use SOS: Self Only Survival skills. For survival, given the intensity of their own needs, the person with ASPD or BPD are busy protecting themselves, responding from a place where even if their response is well-intentioned (i.e., intended to be loving) they actually respond in a self-absorbed way instead of a caregiving way.

In this book, SOS is used to indicate both the person with BPD and ASPD.

Trudi Visits the Nursing Home:

Fifty-three-year-old Trudi rarely visited her father, who was in a nursing home. She finally visited one week. After the visit the ailing father told his nephew he was worried about Trudi. When Trudi visited him she was "down in the dumps," saying she missed her dead mother and that she was struggling financially.

Trudi did not know how to give care to others. She had always been taken care of by her dad and had no clue how to be there for him in his time of need. She didn't understand he missed his wife, too, and could do nothing to help at this point in his life. Trudi would visit, bemoan her own problems, and did nothing to help him sustain his own spirits at the end of his life.

Trudi, as someone with BPD, never developed the ability to be a caregiver. Let me make a distinction between caretaking and caregiving. Caretaking is to take care of, but often caretakers take care of others ultimately for reasons that feed themselves not the other. Caretakers often do not recognize the separateness between self and other. By not recognizing this separateness, they often deplete themselves and end up taking care *from* the other, not taking care *of* the other.

Caregivers, on the other hand, recognize those boundaries and have the ability to recognize needs of the other person, separate from their own needs. They freely give care in a way that nourishes and meets the needs of the other. In recognizing boundaries they have the ability to recognize their own needs so they, themselves, do not get depleted and do not end up depleting the person for whom they are giving care.

The idea of being a caregiver gains more importance when dealing with someone with a personality disorder. When a family member attempts to caretake such a person, it ultimately does not work. There are many examples in this book where the caretaker did not recognize that the person with a personality disorder needed to meet his own needs, solve problems, and develop life skills. In the process the caretakers needs are abandoned.

In order to be in a relationship with an adult with BPD or ASPD it is vital to not caretake but to caregive. To do so you must gain an understanding of how the illness works instead of entering into the hypnotic trance in which the BPD or ASPD person wants you. To aid in your ability to recognize the trance, there will be several later examples of how family members became entranced.

While I do not specialize in seeing clients with BPD or ASPD, I do usually see their family members.

The psychology world knows much about BPD and ASPD, but our profession in general has had a difficult time diagnosing personality disorder. This is partially due to the stigma the diagnosis has traditionally carried. Many psychologists see such a diagnosis as extreme and, likely, hopeless. Other times misdiagnosis has resulted because of the lack of education many mental health providers have received on personality disorders. In addition, some insurance carriers will not cover treatment for a personality disorder, whereas they will cover treatment for such diagnoses as depression, post-traumatic stress, bipolar or attention deficit disorders. Therefore, some clinicians will use these diagnoses instead. It is important to realize that a diagnosis of depression or post-traumatic stress may also be accurate, but to use them alone for a person with BPD or ASPD does not give the whole picture and may lead to less than helpful therapy.

Personality disorders need to be treated differently than depression, etc. For your information, I include the diagnostic criteria used by professionals for both borderline and antisocial personality disorders at the end of this book. There currently are several changes proposed for professionals in these diagnoses and I have addressed those changes as an appendix.

It is well-known among professionals that people with BPD are some of the highest users of mental health services, second only to those with schizophrenia. They also rate high in the use of unemployment and disability services. People with ASPD rarely use mental health services. Research indicates that in the case of BPD there is 69% heritability for the full fledge disorder and 42% for inheriting the traits of the disorder.

Most researchers agree that temperament is the outward face of the disorder. Many believe "kindling," like a stressor or abuse, opens the door for acute symptoms to develop. In one study, borderline symptoms improve over the life span of the person. According to Mary Zanarini, a Harvard clinician and researcher at McLean Hospital, several factors help predict who can improve. Someone who was intervened upon at a younger age, has a good vocational history, has no childhood sexual abuse, and whose family has no history of substance abuse or other personality disorders, like avoidant or dependent, stands a better chance for improvement.

At the University of Minnesota, researchers have found five childhood indicators of a child heading toward BPD:

- a hostile, paranoid world view;
- intense, unstable, and inappropriate emotion;
- overly close relationships;
- impulsivity;
- and a lack of a coherent sense of self (i.e., failure in the identity formation processes).

The researchers believe the difference between BPD and ASPD precursors in childhood is that children who may later develop ASPD are more callous and unemotional and may have physical aggression issues, whereas children who may later develop BPD are overly intimate and may exhibit relationally aggressive tendencies.

Many believe that individuals with BPD seem to be overly fine-tuned to other people. They may interpret some behavior as rejection rather than an indication that the person is simply having a problem of his own. They see the world through a rejection lens. This tendency does not seem to be correlated to a history of abuse, but does seem correlated to an inherent anxiety within the person.

Due to this rejection lens and other reasons, persons with BPD have historically had higher suicidal ideation and threats. Many professionals now think the suicide threats or other harmful manipulative behavior could best be called non-suicidal self-injurious behavior. These attempts may serve the following purposes: escape, avoidance, distraction from their problems, and/or emotional relief.

There are programs created specifically for the treatment of personality disorders. However, many people with a personality disorder will not seek treatment (common with ASPD), or skip through multiple treating professionals (common with BPD). In fact, a history of multiple therapy providers may be one indicator that the person may have a personality disorder.

For people with BPD, being seen as a victim, fragile, or incompetent and needing to be taken care of is part of the profile.

Mary Zanarini believes the focus of the therapy must have several dimensions. The treatment must be aimed at the following:

- temperamental symptoms (i.e., the undue dependence and fearfulness);
- coaching the individual to learn to get around the temperamental symptoms;
- and strategies for both normalizing and adapting to the temperamental symptoms.

The therapy must offer direct help in the social realm. It must also include vocational counseling (i.e., how to look for a job, behave at work, and handle conflict at work). Zanarini believes the program will need to have life coaches who can help the patient with budgeting, cleaning and de-cluttering, doing laundry, standards of personal hygiene, sleep problems, and handling pain. She states her program is designed so the patient becomes open and skillful in the goal of "getting a life." Medication, as she states, "will not give you friends or a job." She is a strong believer in only one medication at a time. Again, these programs are used more with people who have BPD.

Anthony Bateman uses Mentalization-based Therapy (MBT), which involves helping give loved ones a language that is less angry and confrontive. Bateman tries to teach active questioning, saying things to the person with BPD like, "I can see what you're saying. (BPD's impression) but it occurs to me…(alternative impression)." In this stance there is an acceptance of the different perspectives. This emphasizes the need to understand and name the various emotional states in the room. It is essential to keep the discussion in the present. In emphasizing an understanding of the distress in the room, the professional is attempting to lower the person with the ASPD or BPD's arousal state by bringing the person back to the present and the room. In a way, the professional is opening a door for the person with the disorder to ask the question, "What have I done?" The therapist is attempting to get the person with the personality disorder to see what he has done, not simply what has been done to him by a loved one.

The good news is that there are successful treatments for people with personality disorders, although they may need repeat treatment multiple times. The sad news is that many professionals, by focusing on the diagnoses of depression, post-traumatic stress, eating disorders, etc., fail to refer their patients to therapists who treat personality disorders. What is successful with a person with only depression will not be successful for someone with a personality disorder. Even when sent to the right place, the therapist who does not include the patient's loving family members in the conversation may become hypnotized by the victim stance. The therapist may not realize that loving family members are being pushed aside and harmed. The individual who has the disorder may actually be abandoning her family, not the other way around. Given that the person with BPD and ASPD has a distorted lens that is used in viewing daily life, she sees life through a lens that emphasizes rejection. Without information from the other family members, the therapist may unintentionally further contribute to the split of the family and contribute to the patient's distortions.

This communication with family members is especially difficult for the therapist to accomplish given HIPPA (Health Information Portability and Privacy Act). If an adult patient does not want to talk to or meet with family members, a therapist may be stuck. However, a therapist can always listen to a family member without making any comment or identifying that the loved one sees them as a therapist. In doing so, they have the best chance of questioning the distortions the patient may have been led to believe are truth. Unfortunately, this listening is a bind for the therapist; simply by listening, the therapist may be fired by the client. Entering the world of a family with a member with a personality disorder is similar to Alice entering wonderland, what is up is down and down is up. Frequently, therapists wonder if there is more than one personality in the room.

C. Emotional Dysregulation

Marsha Linehan, creator of Dialectical Behavior Therapy and international expert on borderline personality disorder, would prefer to rename BPD as emotional dysregulation disorder. The person who is suffering from BPD has an inability to regulate or contain their emotions. They demonstrate affective instability. When angry, they rage. When anxious, they feel completely panicked. When sad or disappointed, they are sad and whine incessantly. Remember, these are adults doing this, <u>not children.</u>

Anyone who knows my work on active alert children can see a connection. This is why I work so hard with parents of active alert children to teach their children self-regulation using many techniques—from sensory integration, to fuss boxes, to first and foremost making sure the parent role-models how to handle their own emotions. I do not wish the children I know and love to grow up and develop borderline or antisocial tendencies.

If you have ever known a person with BPD you know what emotional dysregulation looks like. Just think of having to hold the telephone three feet from your ear because you are being screamed at. ASPDs will do that, too, but as a bullying technique. Let me provide a few examples of emotional dysregulation:

> ### Lori and Kelsey:
> Thirty-five-year-old Lori was upset with her sister, Kelsey, for talking to Lori's best friend at a party. Lori was fearful about what was discussed. She called Kelsey the morning after the party. Her twelve-year-old nephew answered the phone and Lori yelled, "Get your f—king mother out of bed and tell her I need to speak to her right now." She then yelled at Kelsey for over thirty minutes about what a piece of sh-- she was without ever asking what was said at the party. Kelsey later reported that she had quietly tried to assure Lori what was said but to no avail.

Janice and Her Son:

Janice was the mother of a seventeen-year-old son. When her son came home late one Saturday Janice smelled his breath and yelled, "You're drunk. Get out of my house and don't come back. You're an alcoholic. I won't have you living here."

The son was a good boy who had not used alcohol before; he was an average student and had made a mistake that night. He paged me in tears. He didn't know where to go. As he put it, "She went off on me." He thought she might have become more reasonable within a day or two, but clearly not at that moment. He knew she loved him, but said, "I just don't know what to do when she's like this."

Unlike these examples, sometimes the rage is not open and expressed. You may experience what has been described as a "silent rage." It is different from a sulk or a pout in that all family members know the member with the disorder is angry and rageful. She does not rage aloud, instead she seethes and glares at other family members for days at a time. In certain family systems this is just as effective as the hissy fit is in others.

Family members may unfortunately become adept at keeping the peace by giving in to the inappropriate demands of the member who rages. When family members are unable to tolerate conflict, such rages become very effective for the member with the disorder to get what she wants. This only reinforces the behavior.

Grandma's Birthday:

Dad called Mom to remind her that the family would be going to Grandma's (paternal grandmother) to celebrate her birthday. He asked that she order a cake with raspberries since those were Grandma's favorite. The family decided to meet at the local deli/bakery for dinner before visiting Grandma. It was the same deli from which the cake was ordered. After dinner, Mom tells the others she would pay the bill as she picked up the pre-ordered raspberry torte. Twenty-four-year-old Chloe began sulking and said, "Raspberry, I really wanted chocolate. I've looked forward to it all day." She got up to stomp off, but Dad grabbed her hand and said, "Mom let's see if we can change the order and get chocolate."

Mom was infuriated; she didn't believe this was very good for Chloe. At that time Chloe was in day treatment for her borderline personality disorder. As Mom related this story to me, she felt crazy; she had ordered raspberry because her husband had asked her to since raspberry was Grandma's favorite. She said Chloe ate one piece of the chocolate cake at Grandma's. They brought it home since Grandma didn't want it, and after several days Mom had to toss it. Chloe hadn't eaten any more.

This is Self Only Survival (SOS) in action. One of the more frustrating things about this emotional dysregulation is that the SOS individual will quickly forget or justify away the event where it is demonstrated. This makes it incredibly difficult for anyone to help the individual with BPD or ASPD to see this trait as dysfunctional. In fact, the SOS individual will probably punish any family member who brings up the behavior.

ement

SOS adults have been granted respect but have not been required to be respectful of others within the family, they are extremely entitled individuals. Entitlement means they are aware of what they believe they deserve or are "entitled to." Yet they are unaware of what they owe to others or how they need to be responsible in order to earn their so-called entitlements. In its worst form it means an SOS individual believes the entire family resources belong to them, not the other members of the family. In their own opinion they are the "prince" or the "princess" of the family system or that they are the "sick" or "helpless" one of the family. They deserve this position not because of any worth they attained or work they did, but instead because they have been the baby of the family, the victim of some real or perceived neglect or abuse, or some other cognitive distortion they hold, for example, a parent giving too much to their sibling. Unfortunately, in some families the parent has neither the strength nor ability to disabuse their child of such entitlements.

> ### Michelle and Tuition:
> Mom and Dad paid for Michelle's tuition for over six years. She had yet to get her bachelor's degree. They'd also paid for her apartment and had given her an allowance. Now Dad was beginning to get impatient. He said she must finish at least her bachelor's degree. Michelle ranted and raved at Dad, saying he had paid for her brother's college when he had obtained his bachelor's. Dad didn't point out that the brother finished in four years. Dad was wondering if what he had said to Michelle was fair. After all, "She is a girl" he stated, "maybe I expect too much."

> ### Laura's Spending Money:
>
> Laura, a twenty-five year old, was invited to join her thirty-year-old sister Jenny and brother-in-law on a spring break vacation. Laura lived at home with her parents and was unemployed. Jenny and her husband invited her to come along, thinking it might be a nice break for Laura and their parents. Laura came, expected Jenny to pay for everything, and constantly stated she had no money as they traveled to see a relative in Florida. Upon arriving, they went to a beach. While there, Laura went shopping and proudly displayed four new swimsuits that cost over $300. Jenny asked, "Where did you get the money?" Laura replied, "Oh Dad gave it to me for the trip."

For many SOS individuals this trait is so ingrained in their personalities that they are unable to fathom that they do not deserve everything they want. Any discussion to the controversy falls on deaf ears.

E. Being the Center of Attention

People with BPD or ASPD like being the center of attention. If the issue is BPD they can be quite dramatic in their pursuit of this position. Below are representative stories of family members who inappropriately act out their need to be the center of attention. Notice that Jack, a father with ASPD, needs to have control of everything, he needs to be right, have the right answer, be the smartest. As Nancy McWilliams in *Psychoanalytic Diagnosis, Second Edition: Understanding Personality Structure in the Clinical Process* states, the core of an ASPD is the defense of omnipotent control of those who surround him. Parents with ASPD constantly demean their co-parent to make them feel inferior and concede to being under control. In this way they are the center of attention, albeit with less drama than someone with BPD. The parent with ASPD must be the center of the child's universe, and the child must be totally loyal to that center.

Natalie and her Mom with BPD:

Natalie, in the fourth grade, very proudly invited her mother Di to come to the end-of-the-school-year play. Natalie lived with her grandmother during the school week as Di had trouble reliably getting Natalie to school on time or helping with homework. Di arrived at school but the play had just ended. Di collapsed on the floor and sobbed. The teachers had to bring Natalie out from behind the stage to comfort her mother.

Families With In-laws Who Have BPD:

As illustrated in the case below, sometimes the person who has the personality disorder (Marjory) is an in-law. I first became aware of this case when an adult couple, Isaac and Betty, had come to see me to try to understand and know how to handle Marjory, who was married to Isaac's brother Tom. Historically, there had been difficulty handling Christmas presents, visits, etc. The difficulties became magnified when the only surviving parent of the brothers died. Settling the estate meant agreeing to the demands of Tom, who was egged on by Marjory. My clients, not wanting conflict, agreed and lost significant money on the sale of land to Tom. It was a difficult decision with lawsuits threatened by Tom if Isaac didn't concede. Shortly after this, Isaac contracted cancer and died a year later.

Marjory attended the funeral and asked Betty how the family would be handled in the processional. Betty explained that the hall was small and the only reserved seats were for her daughter, herself, and the speakers. Most of the attendees were family and they were free to sit anywhere other than the first row. Tom did not come, but Marjory had brought their son. She had her twelve-year-old son sit in the only open seat in the second row. She then sat next to him on the floor in the middle open space between the two sets of chairs. The funeral director told her she could not sit on the floor in the middle because of fire regulations. He pointed out several open seats where Marjory and her son could sit together. She proceeded to raise her voice to the funeral director pointing out her son was Isaac's nephew. She then got up, stomped off, called Tom, complained to him, and then came back in and handed the funeral director her phone to talk to Tom. She had also called her brother, a local attorney, who arrived at the funeral home and threatened to sue the home for mistreating Marjory.

Luckily, Betty and her daughter were in another room with other visitors. All of this was relayed to her later by the funeral director.

A Father with ASPD:

In Jack's reality, he was smarter and more capable than his ex-wife. After all, he was once the CEO of a company. He knew best how to parent his son who had Asperger's Syndrome. In fact, he was sure his son was perfectly normal. He believed his ex-wife coddled his son and treated him like a baby. Jack believed his son just needed to know what was expected of him. Jack lost it one day when his eight-year-old son was overwhelmed and screaming. He picked up his son, shook him, and slapped him several times. His son, big sister, and mom all came into my office to talk about what had happened. Because the boy had several marks on his body, I explained that I was required as a licensed reporter to make a report to child protection. The report, I told them, was not to hurt Dad but to help him understand he needed to get help controlling his anger.

The son returned to my office after child protection visited Dad. He mentioned that Dad told him that he could no longer talk to me. According to Dad, I got him in trouble. Nevertheless, the Dad did not prevent him from coming to my office. I didn't want to put the son further in the middle between Dad and me, so we agreed he would not talk. However, just before this visit his son had found a stuffed dog in the trash behind my office building. From then on when I had direct questions about his life I asked Dumpster, the newly cleaned, stuffed dog. Luckily, both for his son and for me, Dad refrained from such outbursts after that point.

F. Inability to Think from Another's Point of View

SOS individuals are incapable of thinking from another person's point of view. They are so narcissistic or self-absorbed that they are unaware of the damage they do to those around them. When a family member tries to make them aware, they simply state their point of view that the harm is really being done to them. They cannot bring into their consciousness how it feels to be the "other" in their life.

Their brains constantly replay scenarios with them as the victim. It almost seems that their emotional development stops growing at about two or three years old—always a self-absorbed, know-it-all who wants to do everything the way they want. In healthy development the child's brain would further develop over time to accommodate the ability to sit in another person's shoes, to learn how their actions impact others. It is as if this ability does not develop in the person with SOS, perhaps due to abuse, neglect, or trauma, or maybe the "lack of fit" between who their parents are and what the child needs. That is not to say it cannot develop, only that it will take work that this person may not be willing to do. Remember, they function with SOS: self only survival skills. (Keep in mind all people who have BPD or ASPD are narcissistic; however not all narcissists have BPD or ASPD.)

> ### Rose Attending Her Parents' Party:
>
> When Rose's mother and father celebrated their thirtieth wedding anniversary, they threw a party for friends and relatives. One of their family friends was a caricaturist who offered to draw pictures at the party. Early in the evening several family members urged Rose, now twenty-eight-years-old and single, to have one done. He drew one in which, according to Rose, emphasized her pointy chin. Rose, unbeknownst to the artist, had always worried about her pointy chin. She left the party distraught and went home to her apartment alone. Rose hurt her parents by not saying goodbye to them even though they were leaving on a week-long cruise the next day. She paged me feeling quite suicidal, completely unaware of how she had affected her parents or their party.

Seeing Life from Your Son's Perspective:

Lance was in second grade and was unsure about his new school. It turned out he was having trouble making friends. Mom and Dad were in the middle of a divorce. Dad, who used to be a CEO, was unemployed and had been going to school to eat lunch and be with his son at recess almost every day of the week. The school was uncertain. how to handle this. They told me they were frightened of Dad and his reactions. Dad had been in the principal's office several times to complain about Mom. The school believed Dad's presence at recess was interfering with Lance making friends. Dad told me the school loved him being there, and that I was crazy and knew nothing about children

The inability to think from another person's point of view is similar to the entitlement trait in that it is extremely difficult for an SOS individual to hear anything different than what they truly believe. It's as if other points of view cannot exist.

G. Victim-Perpetrator cycle

A person with borderline personality disorder (BPD) has a definition of self as a victim: a victim of physical abuse, sexual abuse, emotional abuse, neglect, an alcoholic parent, a mentally ill parent, etc. It is difficult to determine how many people with the disorder have actually been abused. Some researchers believe at least fifty percent.

Parents who have spent thousands of dollars to help their child get well are bewildered. They recognize they were not perfect parents, but also recognize they were not abusive or neglectful and raised other children who are now healthy as adults. In these parents' eyes, the adult child may be seen as having had a fairly protected and idyllic childhood. They may be unaware of their child's sense of abuse or that their adult child may need to be the sick one in the family.

A person with antisocial personality disorder (ASPD) believes they are a victim of our society's rules and laws, big business, etc. Many people with BPD or ASPD behaviors either come from this victim stance or the other perspective with which they are most familiar: the perpetrator stance. The perpetrator stance involves their bullying of parents, siblings, and children. That bullying may involve excessive rage. The person with ASPD seems to vacillate in their interactions from one stance to the other depending who they are around. When they are in public, talking to a stranger or someone they want to impress (i.e. court, therapists), they can perform well for brief periods. They can, in fact, be quite charming.

Kayla's Treatment of Her Friend:

Kayla, who is thirty-three-years-old, complained and complained to her friend that she had guests coming from out of state and needed help cleaning and decorating her house since Kayla had a knee problem. In other words she used her victim stance to ask for help. Her friend arrived an hour late after having to chauffeur her own children to places before she went to help Kayla. When she arrived, Kayla was very agitated. Kayla had changed from her themes of "I am the victim with knee pain" and "of my friend visiting" to perpetrator who was screaming and yelling. Kayla, as related to me by the friend, screeched and screamed and threw the decorations the friend had brought with her. According to the friend, "She called me every name in the book and virtually threw me out. What do I do?"

The Family Christmas with Joy and Grandma Emma:

Eighty-five-year-old Grandma Emma was celebrating Christmas with several of her children and grandchildren. The twenty-five-year-old grandson, who was the child of Emma's daughter Joy, arrived. Everyone was so excited. Even though he and Joy were always invited, he hadn't attended a family gathering in years since Joy divorced his dad. Joy had made it quite clear she was mad at Grandma Emma because she had not completely cut off her ex-spouse who she said was abusive. Her ex-spouse had continued to hunt and fish with the men of the family as he had been one of their childhood friends. Although Grandma Emma had not cut off all contact with Joy's ex-husband, she certainly had minimized it.

Suddenly Joy arrived and walked in straight to Grandma Emma. She yelled at her that she was not going to get away with this. Joy screamed at her twenty-five-year-old son and told him he had no business there. She screamed at her mother, Grandma Emma, about her belief that she had been abused by her for years and left. The entire family was stunned and didn't know what to say. Christmas felt ruined.

> **Amy's First Christmas Without Mom:**
>
> Amy and her husband were doing the extended families' Christmas dinner. This was to be the first time Amy's family gathered after the death of her mother. Her siblings and father had flown in to do Christmas Day at Amy's house. On Christmas Eve they were all invited to her husband's family home. Amy needed to know if her husband's sister and boyfriend would attend the next day because it meant she needed to set up another table if they did. Amy asked her sister-in-law if she and the boyfriend would be coming. The sister-in-law responded, "I don't know." Amy proceeded to say she would like to know as soon as possible. Amy stated, "I would really appreciate your letting me know. It would be considerate." At that point the sister-in-law angrily stated, "What right do you have to tell me what is considerate?" Then Amy was denounced by her parents-in-law as causing a problem for trying to determine who was coming for Christmas dinner. The father-in-law pulled Amy aside and berated her. Amy had violated a family rule, which was that no one would be allowed to upset the sister-in-law.

This victim-perpetrator thinking is one of the most powerful aspects in an SOS individual's personality. They use it to convince others to come around to their view of the world and to gain control of people around them. This control over other people is often referred to as putting them in a trance.

H. Different Realities: Realities in Which Others are to Blame or in Which They are the Hero

When trying to resolve a problem with a loved one with BPD or ASPD, you must keep in mind they simply do not have the same reality that you do. In their reality they have done nothing wrong, they do not choose to remember their rages; their manipulations are for their survival; they are perfect—*you* are the problem. (I'm OK; you're not OK.)

They cannot recognize their own contributions to family problems. Given their concrete, right-wrong, way of thinking, they are not wrong, so you must be. They then construct a reality that coincides with that perception. They truly believe the reality that they construct.

This belief is why it is so difficult for professionals to diagnose BPD and ASPD. Often, a pattern of instability in the social, love, and work arenas and discrepancies with other family members' stories make the personality disorder known to professionals. Many individuals escape an accurate diagnosis. They manage to convince professionals they have post-traumatic stress disorder (and some do), depression, bipolar disorder, attention deficit disorder, etc. By doing so, the professionals may or may not treat the primary disorder, a personality disorder, which leads to a distorted reality and prevents the person from being able to maintain relationships.

Hannah's Work in the Parents' Home:

Fifty-year-old Hannah lived at home and was unemployed. If you spoke with her she would tell you she'd given up the last decade of her life to take care of her parents. In her mind, the reason she was so worn out was that she was just overwhelmed and exhausted from her caretaking.

If you spoke to Hannah's sister you would learn that Hannah had had free room and board from her parents. That their parents wrote checks to Hannah so she could keep her own car, own telephone line, own computer service, hair appointments, etc. The checks totaled more than $1,000 per month for her upkeep. Hannah's boxes of belongings prevented the family from using the family room. Hannah did not cook. She occasionally drove the parents to a doctor's appointment but only if she felt like it. She did no cleaning or washing clothes for them. According to the father, Hannah's responsibilities were to lock up the house at night and fill the birdfeeders.

Jacci's Reframe of Living With Her Sister:

Jacci went to live with her brother's family after running into trouble at work in another state. Jacci had screamed at her boss and quit. However, her boss, who had been a friend of hers, let her take a medical leave of absence instead. Upon returning to work Jacci was given a job with less responsibility and was very unhappy. Her brother felt badly for her and said she was welcome to live with him, his wife, and teenage son. It was his hope that a new state and a new job might help her restart her life. She had divorced three years before. Jacci moved to her brother's and lived there for seven months. She had free room and board. She rarely did any work in exchange. One time the couple left their son with her for two nights while they took a break.

After four months Jacci found a new job. By the time she moved out of her brother's home, she was barely speaking to him or his family; they did not understand why she was mad at them. She never thanked them for their help over those seven months.

A year later while at a party, Jacci's new friend, when introduced to the brother, said, "Oh you're the one who she came to help." As he explored this with Jacci's friend, he learned that Jacci was telling everyone she gave up a high paying, prestigious position to move there and help with her brother's family. The teen son was out of control and Jacci had been the one who helped get things back on track.

Jacci's brother did not correct the friend, but he came to me completely confused as Jacci had not been much help in the house and their son had not had a problem. However, he did recognize she had helped the one weekend when he and his wife had gone away. His question was: How did Jacci get from here to there?

These stories are about the ability of a person with a personality disorder to change in their minds the story of an event and then relay that new story to others with conviction. I must stress, in each story, the person with the disorder completely believes a reality entirely different from those around her. Another example would have been Jack in the section on being the center of attention. He believed I had gotten him in trouble by reporting him to child protection. He did not believe he was culpable for hurting his son.

I. Addictions: Can't Have Enough Goods or Attention

In our professional diagnostic criteria for BPD, one criterion is a pattern of impulsiveness in at least two areas that are potentially self-damaging: spending, sex, substance use, shoplifting, reckless driving, binge eating, etc. People with BPD who have come into my acquaintance have had problems with bingo, poker, shopping, alcohol use, sex, binge eating, anorexia, and misuse of their prescription medications. Another trait I have noticed in some people is their inability to let go of things. Therefore, they may have problems hoarding, i.e., not throwing away or giving away old things and collecting too many things. This leaves their living environments disorganized and overly crowded. In some cases, the amount of hoarding has led to health issues within the living space.

It has been my experience that people with ASPD will exhibit the impulsive behaviors listed above, including addiction. However, I have not seen hoarding in people with ASPD.

Sylvia as a Person Who Could Not Have Enough:

Sylvia was the middle-born daughter of three girls. She was divorced and teaching out west. Sylvia told her brother and sister that she had attention deficit disorder. She frequently used that as her rationale for her messiness or tardiness on visits home.

As the siblings' mother neared ninety, the mother's health began to deteriorate and she walked with a walker. The brother, a successful businessman, and sister, a retired dietician with her own children and grandchildren, convinced Sylvia to retire from teaching and move back home to Mom's house to help care for her. She retired with her own pension of $3,000 per month.

When Sylvia moved in with Mom, it became clear to her other siblings that her problems were worse than they realized. Two years later there were still boxes everywhere in the house— down the hallway where Mom used a walker, stacked to the ceiling in the garage, on either side of the stairs at the entrance of the house. Nothing was organized. Sylvia had to clear her bed each night before she went to sleep. Sylvia was constantly on e-bay buying more and more. Some boxes hadn't even been opened.

The ninety-year-old mother paid all expenses for the house and the car and took Sylvia out for dinner every night at a restaurant since Sylvia did not cook or buy groceries. The Mom's only request was that she wished Sylvia could cook. She was tired of eating out each day.

As the story continued Sylvia convinced her brother that she was exhausted from taking care of Mom. She asked him to buy a cruise for her so she could go on vacation for a week. Then after he purchased it for her, she said she needed him to pay for separate day-excursions off ship. Sylvia said Mom would pay for one if he would pay for another. He didn't want Mom to have to pay, so he purchased two day-excursions. Then she asked for him to pay for a manicure, facial, and massage for her while on the cruise.

Lisa on Christmas Gifts:

Lisa was thirty-five, unemployed, and living at home with her parents. At Christmas she rarely gave any gifts to her parents or her brother and his family. She was always included along with the parents at her brother's home for Christmas dinner. When there was a present exchange, she always received a gift from his family. Last year, they gave her a beaded necklace that came from a local import boutique. In public, with the family around, she gushed about how pretty it was and how she loved it. A week later when the brother was visiting his parents, Lisa called him aside and stated, "This necklace is cheap and given that a receipt was not included I'm sure it's just a re-gift." He had not known where it was purchased. He later related to me he didn't know what to do so he handed her $20 and said his wife would return the gift. The wife became infuriated at Lisa and at her husband. In a session with the brother and his wife, they decided the best option for future Christmases would be to give Lisa only donation cards to good causes that had been made in her name.

> ### Susan's View of Enough:
>
> Susan had lived at home the last three years. She was thirty-one, and had been a boomerang child. This was the third time she'd moved back since college for one or more years. Susan called her sister on several occasions and told her sister that their dad was being abusive to her. At first this would alarm the sister. However, as time went on, the sister learned that Susan saw her father as being mean or abusive if he said "no" to her. When he did, she went to someone else to complain that he was abusive. (We will discuss the game of triangulation in chapter 2.) For instance, she recently told a friend of the family that her dad was mean to her; he would not let her get another cat while living there. Susan's last cat had cost Dad two thousand dollars in vet bills before the cat died.

In Sylvia's, Lisa's, and Susan's behavior, there will never be enough. Sylvia hoards and does not organize or maintain her living environment. Lisa says, "No matter what anyone does for me it will not be good enough." Susan is not grateful that her father has spent thousands on vet bills, but accuses him of being abusive for not being willing to spend more.

J. Conclusion:

Recognizing a family member with a BPD or ASPD is the first step to deciding what you can do about it. A person with a personality disorder may exhibit any of these traits:

- emotional dysregulation;
- entitlement;
- lack the ability to think from another's point of view;
- perpetuate a repetitive victim-perpetrator cycle;
- have different realities from other family members;
- cannot have enough attention or goods.

Beginning to recognize whether a loved one has BPD or ASPD is the first step toward understanding what you can do to stay out of the trance in which you may find yourself. The next chapter will address how to recognize if your loved one has BPD or ASPD through the games (dysfunctional coping methods) they have learned to play, which they believe are required for their survival.

CHAPTER TWO:

Games They Play to Survive

In order to determine whether a family member has BPD or ASPD, you must familiarize yourself with the games, or dysfunctional coping mechanisms, that these people set up to survive. Let me emphasize that I do not believe that people with BPD or ASPD set out to victimize family members by playing these games. Although it may feel that way to you, they have a mental illness. Their brains distort information. They are attempting to survive all alone in a world in which they do not trust and from which they do not feel protected. Despite that, as a family member you must recognize the games as both destructive to them and to you and you must refuse to play.

A. Playing Odd Person Out: Triangulation as Manipulation

A triangle by its very definition has three sides. Pre-teen girls often find themselves unknowingly playing a game called "Odd Girl Out." It usually involves one girl telling another something bad or wrong about a third girl. Interestingly enough, that same girl might then go to the third girl and tell them something bad about the girl to whom she first spoke. That leaves the girl in the middle perceived by both of the other two as being their friend, and the other two are left in the wings believing something bad about each other.

SOS people become masters at this game. They are the "good ones." They are the heroes in their realities. They continually play people against each other. They always try to appear to be the good one, the loyal one, the helpful one, or the victim of harm from one or another, thus needing protection. The hoped-for result of this game is they get to look good and have no blame for the problems of the relationship. Claiming responsibility, owning up to a mistake, is not an option for an SOS person who has not gained any insight into their own disorder.

David Mays, MD, who works in prison, says the prisoners with ASPD are excellent at convincing therapists that they are getting a bad deal from the legal system, family members, and others.

In the game of triangulation, the skill is to constantly shift the blame or responsibility to another party. It is difficult if not impossible for an untreated SOS individual to own a problem, to state, "I was wrong." The shame within overwhelms them, leaving them looking for someone else to blame. In this game, the SOS person often "becomes" a victim of someone else's wrongdoing. If you are in a relationship with a family member with BPD, you eventually become the source of the wrongdoing and the perceived source of their unhappiness. This dynamic is often referred to as splitting; it splits families and friends from within, causing divisions within systems.

- It's Always Someone Else's Fault

A person with BPD or ASPD is incapable of accepting blame and is therefore excellent at blaming someone else for his own choices. Don't play this game. You do not have to confront him but neither do you have to believe him.

George and Drugs:

George was caught with drugs in his dorm room at college at age twenty-four. The amount of marijuana and cocaine George had in his possession meant he was charged as a dealer. His father, a man of great wealth, hired an attorney to defend his son. The attorney negotiated a deal to have George attend a drug treatment program. However, the prosecutor, the attorney, and George still had to appear before the judge in court. George's attorney had asked

George to remain silent. Before the judge was to sentence George, he asked George if he had anything to say. George stood up and told the judge in an arrogant fashion that he should not receive a sentence as he was innocent and was simply holding the drugs for a friend. At this point the judge revoked the agreement between the attorneys and sentenced George to two months in jail and then mandatory drug treatment. The judge did not like George's attitude.

Marne's Blaming Her Father:

Marne is divorced and was recently fired from her job. She asked her sister if she could move back to her home state and live with her sister's family while she got back on her feet. As she was asking her sister if she could stay with them, the sister suggested to Marne that it was not the best time for her to live with them because her husband was quite ill. The sister suggested Marne move back to their mother and father's home to which Marne had returned twice before. Marne explained that would simply have made her too uncomfortable. As she stated, "Dad owns guns and I can't stay there. I might be unsafe." Marne's sister simply replied, "Yes, those are Dad's hunting rifles. They are locked in the gun cupboard. They have been there your entire life."

Marne was trying to make it Dad's fault for not being able to live with her parents. She was trying to guilt her sister into letting her live with her. Nothing had changed at their parents' house from the previous two times Marne had lived with them.

- Triangulation as Odd Man Out

The first goal in triangulation is to look like the good guy or to get others to see you as the victim. The second goal is to make the other two people in the triangle look bad or look like they are perpetrators in each other's eyes—the bully, the abuser. The second goal often splits or divides the group or family. Again, it is often not a conscious or deliberate act on the part of the person with BPD or ASPD. It is an outcome of their need to be seen as the good one. It is an outcome of their inability to think abstractly: people are either for them or against them.

The person initiating the game tries to make one person side with him and then later have the other person side with him. This is more important than telling the truth. Having people on his side is what makes him feel safe. SOS individuals simply have not developed the ability to think in terms of both/and: people can both be for them and not believe their distortions or not play their games. Remember, when you set a limit with this person, you will often be interpreted as being mean or abusive. You can set the limit kindly and with compassion, but you do not get to control how the SOS person perceives your limit setting.

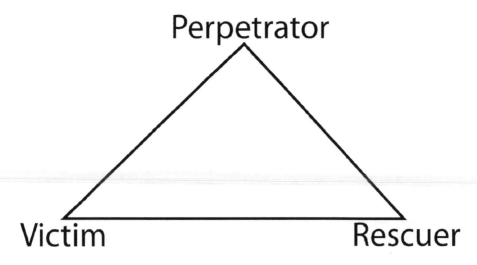

Perpetrator

Victim   Rescuer

Here are some examples of how the triangle works:

○ **Between siblings**

> ### Ada Wanting Boyfriend to Believe Dad Mistreats Her:
>
> Ada was a twenty-four–year-old still working on her bachelor's degree. Ada's boyfriend Carl dropped by Ada's brother's apartment. It was clear Carl wanted to talk. Although Ada's brother and his wife were happy to see him, he didn't usually come without Ada. Carl asked several questions about Ada and the family. It was clear something was bothering him. Carl had been told by Ada that Ada's brother and wife's apartment was paid for by their father. They explained to Carl that was not true. Carl also believed the father paid for the couple to take a trip to Europe last summer. Again they explained to Carl that was not true. Carl was perplexed, he said Ada clearly believed those things to be true. Ada's brother explained that his father had paid his tuition while he was working on his bachelor's degree but had quit paying room and board his second year when he'd moved into an apartment with friends. He was clear that both he and his wife worked and received no financial support from Dad. Carl now wondered why Ada wanted him to believe she was somehow being mistreated by Dad when Dad wanted her to start paying for a portion of her rent? Ada's dad had always paid her rent, and she was angry Dad was asking her to pay some of it now. Carl had come to get the brother to talk to Dad for Ada.

Sue and Christmas as a Time to Divide:

Sue went to her brother's house once or twice a year. She went for a nephew's graduation. She went at Christmas loaded with presents. Sue often stayed four or five days. The house was full of fun and energy. While she was there, Sue constantly criticized their other sister, who lived in the same town, saying she neglected her children.

What the brother didn't realize was that when Sue was visiting the other sister's house she was constantly belittling the brother, his wife, and his teenage son. But he had begun to notice that his sister, who lived in town, seemed to be more and more distant after each of Sue's visits. He knew Sue was fun but also mercurial. As he stated to me, "She's divorced three times and seems to only stay in the same job for two or three years."

I encouraged him to speak alone to the sister who lived in town. However, the danger in doing so was that he may have appeared to simply be putting Sue down just as Sue had done to him. He needed to be careful not to do this. Sue had spent a long time shaping her sister's reality of his family. Just as she had spent time shaping his reality of what their sister's family was like.

It was difficult to undo the many subtle perceptions she may have created within his other sister's mind. Only time and his own behavior would undo the seeds of animosity that had been planted. He needed to always try to be his best and most respectful self when talking to his other sister. In that way she could eventually begin to question within herself what she had been told about the brother by Sue versus her own experience of him.

Gayle's Dividing the Siblings:

Within the family of siblings, Gayle, the baby, had been taken in by both her brother's and sister's families at various times in her life after divorce, job changes, etc. Each time she lived with them a few months, then left in a huff barely speaking to whichever sibling she had been living with. This time she was back at her sister's home. They had another half-brother who lived in the same city as the sister.

Gayle was thirty-seven and loved to shop and have fun; so did the half-brother's wife. This time the sister, who was my therapy client, reported that Gayle spent more and more time over at the half-brother's. "Gayle seems to have developed a social life through his family. She seems to be there most evenings or goes out shopping with his wife. It's really nice she's made this connection." The problem was that the sister used to have a good relationship with this half-brother's family. Now she reported that she thought her half-brother was pulling away from her and her family. She believed the half-brother's wife was being negatively influenced by Gayle.

On several occasions I have seen the person with BPD align with an in-law. The in-law of the family of origin system then seems to influence the spouse, child, or sibling to distance from his original nuclear family. Siblings who had at one time been close have grieved the loss of that sibling in my office, feeling powerless to counter what is happening.

○ **Between siblings and parents**

When the person with the disorder is in the sibling group, the pattern I have most often observed is one in which another adult child develops more into a hero, i.e., the responsible one, the reliable one.

Noel Larson, a psychologist who specializes in personality disorders and abuse, uses the term "overachiever victim" to describe this hero role because the hero is also a victim. A hero works hard to achieve, to be responsible, to function, to not be like her sibling.

If this is your role you probably did not learn to listen to your own needs. The other sibling, the one with BPD, becomes more and more typecast as the victim—that is, the "ill" one, the trauma victim, the "incapable" one. He or she is frequently codependent with one parent. Codependency is an unhealthy relationship that involves the parent caretaking in ways that harm the relationship and growth of the child.

In families with more than two siblings there might also be the disconnected one, more than one hero, or more than one victim. What affects the roles the siblings play the most is what the parents do with the disorder. Do they ignore it and try to pretend all is well? Do they enable the person with the disorder?

Sasha's Medications:

Sasha came to a party at her cousin's house with her parents. Sasha had taken too many anxiety medications. When the cousin pointed out that Sasha was over-medicated, Sasha's Mom replied, "Sasha's had a hard day." The cousin asked me if Sasha's mother really believed it was alright for her daughter to go around over-medicated. She thought it was dangerous. However, the Mom, who was codependent with her daughter, justified the medication choice.

• No-talk rule

You've probably noticed families that seem to struggle the most with an SOS family member function with a no-talk rule. The point is the SOS family member will only be thinking of herself and may explicitly or implicitly ask other family members not to talk. In the following examples, in the case of Michelle the request was very explicit; in Ellen's case it was just understood.

Michelle's Bills:

Michelle had run up many different bills and found herself in debt at age twenty-eight. She wrote her grandmother a letter asking for financial assistance. In the letter to Grandma, Michelle clearly wrote that Grandma should keep the request only between Michelle and herself. Grandmother brought the letter to me asking for advice, because she was uncomfortable keeping the request a secret. She knew her son had given Michelle financial help and she wondered if it would be helpful or harmful to give Michelle money.

Ellen's Medications:

Ellen had a personality disorder and was on several medications. Her children saw me. Her son was very confused because his mother seemed to be sick and slept a lot. As we were playing, I simply stated that Mom took certain medications and the doctors were changing them. The medicines were affecting the amount Mom slept. The doctors and Mom were working on getting it right. I told him it was an adult problem and she had many helpers. I assured him it would be better soon.

He was very relieved. I knew about the medication change because Mom had informed me. However, she had not informed me the family never talked about her use of medications. Although her son felt better, Ellen came in infuriated the next week that I had told her son she took medicines. I had to explain that her son, who was eight, was very aware that she took medicines as he had seen all the bottles, even though she had never talked about it to him.

Joseph's Sabotage of His Son's Therapy:

Joseph was a father who I believe had ASPD. He had tried frequently to sabotage my relationship with his son. From my perspective, he felt threatened by anyone: a teacher, an aunt, a therapist—anyone who might give his son any view of reality that Dad did not believe. Joseph frequently questioned the son about whether I really listened to him, whether I made fun of him, or made him uncomfortable in some way. In my office all people are safe and accepted. I frequently had to help his son remember what his experience with me was different than what Dad was telling him it was. It was very confusing to the son to experience being heard and then to be told by his Dad that he was not heard.

Joseph talked to his son but did not want his son to talk with anyone other than himself.

○ **Between children, parents, and grandparents**

In more recent years I have had grandparents in my office who are raising grandchildren. The person with BPD or ASPD is the grandparent's adult child or their adult child's ex-spouse. Sometimes the person is living with the grandparents and grandchildren; sometimes they are not.

If you are a child growing up with grandparents it may be hard to understand why your mommy or daddy can't be there for you. In the case of a parent with ASPD who has been arrested for dealing drugs, it may be easier because she is in jail. However, the damage done before the child is placed with the grandparent may be enormous. This includes damage due to triangulation between the grandchild, parent, and grandparent. The parent may have spent years telling her child not to trust the grandparent. She did this so the child would not talk about how she was left alone or how the grandchild needed to even fix her own food. Then, suddenly, the grandparent becomes the very person the grandchild has to trust since the parent cannot parent because she is incarcerated, or the parent and child have to move back into the grandparents' home for financial reasons.

> **Ginny Living With Grandmother:**
>
> Ginny came to me as a six-year-old. She was brought in by her grandmother. Ginny was very mature for her age. She had been asked by her mother to take care of her four-year-old brother on many occasions. Those many occasions occurred because mom left to score her drug of choice, meth. Ginny was proud that she could prepare food, change diapers. She even once showed me how she could take down a big man if he was going to try to hurt her or her brother. However, Ginny could not answer any questions or talk about her own feelings. She did not understand feelings—that she could be mad or scared or sad. Ginny was confused because now she was living with Grandma and Grandpa. Ginny's mom had told her on many occasions not to tell Grandma that Mom left her alone to take care of her brother. Mom had told her Grandma wouldn't understand how smart Ginny was. There were many secrets Mom had expected her to keep.

If you are grandparents and have the person with BPD or ASPD living with you, a different problem occurs. The grandparents who want the best for the grandchildren do the work of childcare, helping with homework, and putting them to bed. However, the grandparents are in constant fear their son or daughter might take the grandchildren and remarry or leave. They know their son or daughter does not demonstrate many parenting skills. They want their adult child to become independent but not at the expense of their grandchildren. Although the grandparents may be the primary custodians and provide all the stability for their grandchildren, they do not have parental rights or legal custody.

Grandparents' Fears:

The first member of the Jones family I met was Grandma. Both she and Grandpa were teachers in a local school system. Retirement normally would be in two years. They were not sure they could afford to retire. Their son and their two beautiful grandchildren lived with them. Their son worked, but only part-time as an apprentice carpenter. Sometimes he worked one day a week, sometimes three. He said he couldn't work more given his low seniority ranking with the Union. Grandma and Grandpa had raised his children, doing the cooking, the washing, homework, and nighttime routines. The children were four and six. They had lived with the grandparents for over three years. The son and his wife had an expensive, conflict-ridden divorce for which the grandparents paid. Mom had been a drug user according to the son. Mom only had periodic weekend visitation with her children.

Grandma was concerned about the family's future. The children had no health insurance. They got constant calls on the home telephone from her son's creditors. He dated and brought women home to meet his children right away in each new relationship. Grandma was worried he might impulsively marry one of them and take the children and leave. The son said they were all picking on him and he wouldn't come to family therapy. Remember, people with ASPD seldom seek treatment.

○ **Between and with professionals**

> ### Trisha and Visitation:
>
> Trisha was seven when I met her many years ago. Her parents' attorneys had both suggested I work with Trisha and her parents. The attorneys asked me to expedite visitation. The parents had divorced four years before and were still arguing about everything related to Trisha. During my play sessions with Trisha, she made it clear to me that she enjoyed being with her dad and would like a little more time with him. Any variation in the visitation schedule caused enormous battles between the parents. Dad asked if he could bring Trisha back by 7:00 p.m. on Sundays in the summer because he often took her to the family cabin three hours away for the weekend. The normal exchange time was 6:00 p.m. Given that there was no school, I encouraged the parents to make the change for the summer, thereby honoring Trisha's and her father's request for more time.
>
> The next day Trisha was marched into my office and stated, in words no seven-year-old uses, "Clearly you misunderstood Dr. Budd. I don't want any more time with my Dad." Trisha had been coached. She called me Linda when we played. She was obviously under great stress. Mom then asked Trisha to leave the room and told me neither she nor Trisha had any more need for my services.

The last I heard, Trisha at age thirteen had run away from her mother's house to her father's. She was on antidepressants. Dad returned to me and asked if I could help protect Trisha from her mother, whom I had suspected as having borderline personality disorder years before. Mom was trying to force Trisha to return to her home. Dad's fear was that Mom would misuse or attack Trisha's current therapist. I agreed to speak to Trisha's therapist and then wrote a letter to the attorneys so Trisha's therapist would not be placed in a destructive triangle.

In the example above, I worked with the other therapist so she would not become part of a destructive triangle. In other examples, therapists have become quite angry with one another. One therapist believed the reality of the person with the personality disorder; one believed the other parent. It is vital for therapists to question why such discrepant realities are in the family or the therapist becomes another pawn in the triangle and are not helpful.

For those of us who have worked in the field, we have a saying, "If two professionals working with various members of the same family start arguing about reality, look for a family member with a personality disorder." To simplify, the person with BPD or ASPD will tell their therapist one reality; whereas, the therapist of the parent, sibling, or spouse will be told a completely different reality. Yes, people with personality disorder are experts who can even triangulate professional therapists if those therapists are not careful.

> ### Lisa's Perceptions:
>
> Lisa was forty-five and lived at home with her elderly parents. Once, when both parents had become sick, she called 9-1-1 to complain that she was suicidal since she had so many responsibilities in caretaking her elderly parents. The paramedics came to the house and took suicidal Lisa to the hospital where she remained for a week. The hospital, not knowing any other part of the story, placed her in a support group for caretakers. Lisa's sister came in my office and said, "This is ridiculous. Mom asked her to do one load of laundry that day and fix them some soup since Mom was sick. Lisa is far from any kind of caregiver. They caretake her."

With the advent of HIPPA, professionals are no longer free to share information about the various members of a family without each one's written consent. It would be highly unlikely that an SOS person would allow a release of information to a family member whose views they suspect would conflict with their own view of reality or a release to a therapist of another family member for the same reason. Remember, in her mind, Lisa's sister is simply mean to her and does not understand how difficult her life is. Keep in mind that although the therapist may not talk to a family member, they can listen to a family member without a release.

The next place this use of triangulation becomes important is with the court system. A person with BPD or ASPD can look quite charming in public for limited public appearances. They completely believe the reality they have created inside their brains. They are entitled and believe they should have control in their families due to their own anxieties about the other members of the family. Therefore, they frequently manipulate court systems to maintain control. An ASPD father can and has often gotten full physical custody of his child despite the best interests of the child. The judge may even have before him medical data showing the child has been abused or molested and testimony from the child that the father is the perpetrator. The judge is often caught between believing the data or believing what appears to be a very sincere father.

A high-functioning BPD parent will tie the court in constant litigation over physical custody of the children. That parent can present well to her attorney and in court. In the case of Trisha, her mother's attorney contacted me after I wrote a letter supporting Trisha's move to her father's home at thirteen. The attorney reminded me that I could not state such an opinion because I was the visitation expeditor of record. I had to call the attorney to tell her the mother had fired me from that role six years before. Obviously, Trisha's mother failed to report the action of firing me to her attorney.

Finally, the nature of an SOS individual is they do not like boundaries and interpret them as simply being mean or abusive. Therefore, a person with a personality disorder may have a long list of therapists they have seen and fired. They then may have used triangulation by reporting those therapists to their professional boards for perceived violations. In this way, the Board becomes the third part of the triangle with the person with ASPD or BPD trying to convince the Board they are the victim of the licensee. It is always important to handle such people with the utmost care and the clearest of boundaries, and for professional boards to recognize the pattern.

B. CWC: Complaining, Whining, and Criticizing

Complaining, whining, and criticizing (CWC) are all tools used by an SOS person to divert attention back upon themselves and to get their way with the intent of controlling the other person. By complaining, whining, or criticizing they try to make others change in order to make something (i.e., the situation) more to their own liking. What is consistent is the nature of how they try to make a change. They don't work at change; they work at making others change things for them. Criticizing is powerful. Their families might comply with their wishes, simply to avoid conflict. Unfortunately, given that rarely is a situation good enough for them, parents end up placating and subsequently reinforcing the SOS person's destructive traits. Parents and others give in or make changes simply to avoid conflict or try to make the person to whom they're connected happy. This allows the SOS family member to control the family without limits.

Lila's Absence from the Party:

Nineteen-year-old Lila returned home as her family was finishing celebrating her sister-in-law's birthday. Mom explained that Lila had left that morning without saying where she was going or how long she would be gone. Mom said Lila didn't take her cell phone and was unreachable. As Lila entered the home and saw the party almost over, she yelled at all in attendance, "You ate lunch and allowed her to open her presents without me! What, I am not part of the family?" She proceeded to scowl and finally went into her room to pout.

Mom followed Lila to her room and, feeling sorry that she had missed the party, gave her $20 to go shopping and eat lunch out. Then Lila left the rest of the family to go out for lunch.

When I heard this, I wondered whether Lila really missed being with the family or simply used her blow-up to make her mother feel guilty and to hopefully make up for the perceived guilt with money.

When living with a person who constantly criticizes everyone else you may become very anxious. The anxiety stems from not wanting to do things wrong lest you also become the focus of your family member's criticism. It affects all your decisions. You may even hand over decisions to the sick family member simply to avoid criticism. That, in essence, leaves the SOS family member in charge. You are at their mercy. Given that, by the very nature of the illness, an SOS individual is self-absorbed; she has little mercy. It can go so far as to make you a victim in your own home.

This dynamic of giving away your responsibility in order not to be criticized places you at risk for anxiety, depression, and, worse yet, supporting and paying for your own victimization. This denial of self's needs in order to please others is codependence. It is often found between another family member and the SOS individual. Remember, there will not be enough for an SOS person, therefore you are choosing to forever remain in the service of an SOS's whims.

It is dangerous for other members of the family and results in a terribly unhealthy family dynamic. If other family members have the ability to handle conflict, it leaves them in an impossible dilemma. They are left to negotiate with a mentally ill family member as if that person is capable of placing other family members' needs first. The mentally ill family member, who does not have this capability, is given far too much power. See Peter's Story in chapter 6 for an example of such a family dynamic.

C. Projecting what the SOS person is actually doing or thinking

Projecting is accusing *you* of doing or thinking what the *SOS person* is actually doing or thinking. Imagine having a conversation with your SOS family member when they are dysregulated, that is, emotionally unstable or even explosive. Throughout the conversation they will forcefully accuse you of being dysregulated (e.g., doing the very thing they are doing). By doing so, they are saying "I'm OK; you're not OK." It has been described to me as the ultimate in crazy making: "It's almost as if she takes the steam out of any negative feedback I might have for her by telling me that is not what she is doing. In fact, she says that is really what I'm doing." "It's like I just went through the hole in *Alice in Wonderland*. What's up is really down. I feel crazy. I can't get my bearings."

The truth is that negative feedback is extremely difficult for an SOS individual. A better approach is to think about what you can change in your own behavior and ask for any change as a wish, not an expectation, in your kindest, most respectful manner. Always keep in mind you can only really change yourself, not the SOS family member.

Iko and Money:

Iko constantly accused her sister Luann of using their parents just for their money. Of course the opposite had been true. All of Iko's life, Iko's parents had bailed her out of one situation or another.

Luann was a business professional who had borrowed part of a down payment from her parents when she first purchased her home but had paid it back to them within a year. Luann borrowed again seven years ago, but the parents said they did not want to be repaid given their numerous payments to Iko.

Iko repeatedly referred to this when accusing Luann of using their parents for their money. Iko had taken many thousands of dollars from her parents but insisted they were gifts, whereas the money Luann borrowed, according to Iko, was a loan. Luann helped the parents repeatedly get to appointments or made dinners for the family. Iko never did. But Iko still accused Luann of using their parents only for their money.

Chrissy and Her Brother:

Chrissy yelled at her brother that he was being nosey. However, their mother, upon the death of their father, had asked him to help her understand the finances. Understanding the finances meant going through the cancelled checks. During the process, he learned how much money the parents had given to Chrissy over the past few years. He told his Mom that she would no longer be able to afford to give Chrissy so much money. Chrissy called him that evening and yelled for over an hour that he had no business telling Mom not to give her money. During the phone call, it became clear that Chrissy had known for years how much money Mom and Dad had given his family. She knew the exact amount their mother had given him, his wife, and his children for Christmas and birthday presents. He, however, had not known anything about the situation with Chrissy until his mother asked him for help. His mom was asking him for help, but Chrissy told him he was nosey for giving that help. He came into my office to figure out what to do.

While these examples were centered on money, projecting isn't done just around the issue of money. It can be around any issue, for example, being accused of yelling at an SOS family member when it's really the SOS family member doing the yelling. Another common occurrence happens at the death of the parent. I have heard stories about very dishonest siblings stealing things from the parents' estate and accusing the honest sibling of stealing. It serves the purpose of making the more honest sibling be that much more open and explicit about his actions. That openness is then used by the SOS sibling to loot the estate while others aren't looking. The internal justification of the SOS sibling is usually that the honest sibling is doing the same thing behind his back. It seems as if she cannot believe in anyone's honesty while acting dishonestly.

- Triangulation while projecting

It can get even crazier. When arguing and projecting to you what they truly believe is your problem, the SOS family member will inevitably create a triangle. In the argument they will say things like "I've talked to our brother and he believes you really have an X problem (name the problem)."

50

The SOS person may invoke another family member, their therapist (whom you must understand only has the SOS person's point of view), or a long-dead ancestor.

It is important to realize they may be lying, or at best practicing a form of wishful thinking. They may have taken some small comment out of context and used it for their own purposes. If you are concerned, you may need to go to the person, if alive, whose name is being invoked to check out if the perception or statement has truth. The truth may be far different from what is being reported. Remember, the pattern is to distort for their own survival, which in turn splits the family. They say negative things about other family members and do not take responsibility for their own actions.

D. Somatizing

Somatizing means that instead of dealing with feelings, one's feelings come out in physical conditions. Particularly, SOS individuals with BPD will be ill with one thing or another. Most, if not all, of the illnesses are not serious or life threatening. They may be a bit uncomfortable, but the illnesses become completely consuming to them and, they hope, to all those around them. Remember, the SOS person is a victim. That includes being the victim of their own bodies. They use their illnesses to maintain their position as the center of attention. Any pain at all is a 10 on a 10-point scale.

To be fair, there are some people who, due to sensory overwhelm, are much more sensitive and aware of their own bodies. Sensory defensive disorder and overwhelm is the tendency not to be able to screen information coming into the body and through the body. It is important to learn coping skills for sensory defensiveness. Occupational therapists do an excellent job of helping children develop those coping skills with work that was begun by Jane Ayres, an occupational therapist and developmental psychologist. There are others who, because of the abuse they experienced, maintain memories of that abuse in their bodies, which then appear as a physical symptom.

This tendency to be sick can also become part of the family system. The SOS family member may, due to anxiety, not feel like coping and may take on the role of the "sick" one or the "needy" one of the family. As a parent, you must learn not to reinforce this role. During childhood, parents must emphasize, as Eleanor Roosevelt once said, that most of the people at work on any given day are not feeling their best. Life goes on. Miriam Hey, a master teacher, said, "Children need sometimes to learn to get over it."

Many SOS individuals become malingerers. They may even get fired from their jobs for missing so much work because of illness. They may go on social security disability after many years of proving they cannot function in the world of work. However, there are SOS individuals who are high functioning. Certain work environments help them to hide better.

An SOS person's tendency to be sick is one of their ways of trying to remain the center of attention. Since they do not gain attention for positive accomplishments, it is *not* a big leap for the SOS person to work at being the best incompetent or sick person in the family. If given too much empathy when sick, it is understandable that an SOS person sticks to that role instead of trying to deal with the anxiety about the fear of functioning. A problem arises when another member of the family becomes seriously sick. The SOS family member does not take well to having the sick role usurped. Sometimes they will do something to regain the role, i.e., like threaten suicide. Remember my story of Lisa when both parents became sick. Lisa called 9-1-1 to say she was overwhelmed and suicidal.

> ### Kelsey's Real Illness:
> Kelsey was afraid. She told her brother John that she had been scheduled for more tests by her doctor because an earlier test indicated some abnormal cells. John mentioned this to his wife Georgia. Georgia was close to John and Kelsey's SOS sister, Madison. Georgia and Madison decided there was really no problem. Madison triangulated the siblings since a real illness would have taken attention away from her. Madison informed John and Georgia that she had had tests like this all the time. It was no big deal. John went back to Kelsey. He didn't bother to ask the medical facts, but said to her, "Georgia and Madison say your tests are no big deal."

> Kelsey came into my office and decided she had two choices: 1) either try to get them to understand what was really happening and be supportive, or 2) quit asking for their support and use her friends to support her through treatment instead. She went with the second option since she said she didn't have the energy to work so hard to get support.

E. Ideas, Ideas, Ideas Versus Work

An SOS individual has usually found some incredible ways of coping, albeit dysfunctional, by the time they are adults. Many of the people I have met are very bright, creative individuals. Their coping mechanisms are quite creative, although destructive, for them and for those who love them. The ones who are high functioning will be filled with creative ideas—ideas that within the family are ultimately narcissistic and meant once again to place them at the center of attention.

Although they are often wonderful ideas, they expect other family members to do the work of getting the idea to a real product. Remember, these people have trouble with self-regulation, in other words, self-discipline. As a family member working with an SOS person, it is best to decide in advance if the idea is worth your effort, since it will mostly be your effort that will bring the project to fruition. As is often said in the addiction field, "they can 'talk the talk' they just can't 'walk the walk.'" With an SOS individual, follow-through is, at best, inconsistent and, at worst, non-existent.

Briah and Susan:

Two sisters, Briah and Susan, wished to honor their parents' 50th wedding anniversary. Briah had the idea to throw the parents a party even though she didn't live in the same town as Susan and her parents. Briah and Susan decided to send out invitations to all the parents' friends and relatives. Briah was great at coming up with the list to invite and said each person should bring a picture or something that represented a memory of good times together.

Briah flew in two days before the party in order to help. However, Briah kept leaving to go out places and shop for herself. Susan asked for help, but Briah always said "later." Thirty minutes before the party was to begin, Briah came in from shopping. Susan had decorated the house, picked up the food and, because she was not ready, asked Briah's help to place the food on the table. Briah blew up and stated, "I knew you would be like this," and ranted about how Susan's attitude would wreck the party.

Briah was delightful at the party and talked to everyone saying how hard she'd worked to honor their parents.

Susan said Briah left the next morning. Susan then had to spend hours putting together the memory book for her parents that was supposed to be the gift from Susan and Briah. Although resentful, she was clear the party and the book had been worth her effort. She also thought it was important for her parents to believe that Briah and she had worked together on their behalf.

This concept of ideas and lack of follow-through is intricately connected to the CWC (Complaining, Whining, and Criticizing) game referred to earlier. Another variation of CWC is the "blame the person who does the work" game. This occurs both at work and at home. If the SOS individual can deflect the issue away from their lack of participation in doing the work to some other issue, they win. Notice Briah's deflection away from the issue of her participation in preparation toward Susan's attitude. Briah does not at all accept responsibility for helping in the preparations.

This game is also played at work, which is why it's difficult for the SOS individual to remain employed at one place for very long.

F. Employment

As stated earlier, a low-functioning SOS person has difficulty with employment and may end up on disability. People who have this disorder but are higher functioning often change jobs every few years, often because they are fired or demoted. The SOS person is as adept at triangulating at work as they are within the family. Within large companies they may be moved from one division to another in order to solve the personality problems they create within the division.

High-functioning SOS people may start their own business. They may become a computer consultant, run their own landscape business, become an independent lawyer, an interior decorator, a therapist, etc. They handle the world of work much better from the position of boss given their need to control. However, their employees or underlings may feel the brunt of the SOS person as boss. If the SOS individual does have a manager, that person may need to allow such coping mechanisms as working from home periodically and allowing for more illness than usual as an exchange for the good ideas the SOS contributes to the workplace.

Conclusion:

The consistent pattern is that the life of an SOS individual is inconsistent. Jobs change. Friends change. The SOS person always has an explanation for their changes, such as the unethical behavior on the company's part, the alcoholism on the friend's part, the lying on the ex-spouse's part, or the spouse's philandering. The changes are the result of someone or something else being bad or wrong. Sometimes they say they are not a victim but instead a hero; for example, they change jobs because they are offered a significant raise. However, the one consistent variable is the SOS person. They are the only common factor in all the jobs, the marriages, the friends. They will work at trying to convince family members that they are either a victim of others' wrongdoing or an incredible hero. In fact, they truly believe they are a hero for not condoning a company's misguided policies by quitting or they are a victim by continuing to work for such a corrupt institution.

If you have a relationship with this person, remember an SOS will work to put you in a trance. You will be seduced by his voice, his looks, etc. You will willingly offer to take responsibility for him. You will protect him. You may even pay his bills for him or loan him money. People who are most easily seduced by an SOS person are those who are caregivers by nature, those who are more anxious and less certain of their own worth, those who give away their loyalty and make no demands in return (like a codependent), and finally, those who can be seduced by the stroking of their ego. Remember, an SOS needs their victims and are excellent for short periods of time at presenting to us what we might need so that, in the long run, they gain what they need for survival.

To exit the trance, you must do a self-evaluation. Remember, the SOS person is only feeding you what he perceives you desire or fear. Be wary of those who place you on a pedestal and/or throw you in the trash. It is important to take stock of your own needs and develop a plan to meet them through your own actions. Self worth is located within you; it does not come from others. You must learn to see the truth of others and speak the truth to yourself.

CHAPTER THREE

What Contributes and What Helps

The patterns of behavior of a person with BPD and ASPD are important to recognize. It is also important to understand some contributing factors that exacerbate the traits that lead to being an SOS. This chapter provides insight into these factors and some helpful paths to diminish the power of an SOS within the family.

A. Contributing Factors

Following all the tales and the research, let me reiterate that there are certain factors that contribute to the development of a personality disorder. First and foremost, if a person with a more sensitive temperament is abused or neglected there is a higher likelihood of developing SOS skills.

We know that some children with certain gene variants may be very sensitive to a "lack of fit" between how their parents handle them and their perception of that process. David Dobbs, author and journalist, is currently working on a book called *The Orchid and the Dandelion*. In an article written for *New Scientist* he discusses orchid genes, which contribute to how sensitive children are to the way they are parented. Children with 4 or 5 orchid genes are most affected by their upbringing. With good parenting the children are well behaved; with poor parenting the children become difficult. Children with 0 or 1 orchid genes, which Dobbs refers to as dandelion children, behave about the same regardless of their home life, doing fine no matter their surroundings. These orchid gene variations only cause problems when combined with a difficult childhood. Even with the gene variations, children who are parented well are even more likely to share with another child than those without these gene variations. It seems the orchid gene variations lead the child to either be more compassionate or more of a bully, depending upon how they are parented.

Another contributing factor to the development of a personality disorder is parental discord or division. This occurs when parents either do not know how to work as a parenting team or war with each other and sabotage the child's relationship with the other parent. The war may mean that one of the parents is unable to see the child's life from the child's perspective. Such parent(s) may have the traits of a personality disorder or a full disorder. When a parent has personality disorder, they are unable to role model the ability to count another's needs, and they are unable to role model self-discipline or the necessity to follow rules or order.

A parent or significant family member with a history of addiction or personality disorder also contributes to the development of a personality disorder. Both addiction and personality disorder change the parenting dynamic. It is obvious that a parent with a personality disorder will model poor coping strategies to a child who may have inherited the traits. However, the dynamic can be more subtle. Sometimes it is not a parent but a grandparent who has the personality disorder. The parent may have grown up with a parent with the disorder and became very adaptable to the craziness in the relationship, more or less codependent with their parent. Subsequently, when that child grows up and has children he is too adaptable to the personality disorder traits within his own child. The child is a gift, or new opportunity, to learn the need and importance of personal limits.

Edward John Bowlby, a British psychologist and child developmentalist, developed a theory of attachment. Anthony Bateman, a British psychologist, describes one source of borderline personality disorder using Bowlby's attachment theory. Bateman says a disorganized attachment between caregiver and child seems most important in the development of BPD. A disorganized attachment is one in which the attachment figure (or caregiver) is simultaneously a source of both reassurance and fear.[1]

[1] The relationship between a preoccupied or disorganized attachment and BPD has been found by Lyons-Ruth (2005).

As for drug, alcohol, sex, work, gambling, or food, the family dynamic of addiction usually includes a no-talk rule and high denial. It often also includes the other parent being codependent and enabling the addiction. It is a very small step to move from enabling an addiction to enabling the traits of a personality disorder. We have already addressed how enabling is not helpful with personality disorders. I believe this is one of the reasons Al-Anon, an organization for the partners of alcoholics, has been useful to people whose family member has a personality disorder.

Another consideration would be other environmental stressors that contribute to the development of the disorder, which include the exposure to physical or sexual abuse as a witness, or the perception or reality of abandonment, when a child has been orphaned or left in foster care.

Finally, in our world we must include the small portion of children who have witnessed other trauma, such as a killing or a terrorist event. All of the above may lead to a personality disorder, we simply do not know enough.

B. Helpful Paths

The distortion that love conquers all, heals all, is not true. This will be further discussed in the chapter on lessons to be learned. However, we need to define love in order to determine what the possibilities really are. In my book *The Journey of Parenting*, I discuss the four elements a parent must provide in order for a child to feel loved. They are: security, protection, importance, and respect. In the book, I try to help parents understand there are consequences for providing too much or too little security, providing the child with too much or too little protection, helping a child feel either too important or not important enough, and granting the child too much or too little respect. I discuss the need for parents to remain "in the channel," that is, to remain between the two extremes.

In my clinical experience I have had the pleasure of knowing and observing so many children who begin life with temperamental traits. These traits, if allowed to run amok, could have ended up with a personality disorder; however, in the vast majority of cases the traits did not. In my book *Living with the Active Alert Child*, I talk about handling children who had previously been called "difficult." I am a believer that parenting in infancy and beyond can and does make a difference. I am in <u>no</u> way saying parents cause personality disorder, although this may be the case if they are the child's abuser or neglectful of the child. What a child brings to us at birth, whether we call it temperament or personality disorder traits is a given, they are no one's fault—neither child nor parent. There are children who, due to neglect, (e.g. an ill sibling or an ill parent), real abandonment (e.g. orphaned), physical or sexual abuse, or other trauma experience, tip the scales toward personality disorder. A parent at best may only dampen the severity and steer them ever so lovingly back into the channel. When the child grows up in a loving environment with parents who just know too little about limits, who may have some problems but are not abusive or neglectful, it is my belief that active parenting can shift the child back within the channels and yield better outcomes for his adult life.

In over 35 years of my work with children that I have referred to as active alerts, and other professionals may refer to as a difficult temperament, I have seen only a small minority become personality disordered. Why? I believe the parents were working with a model whose structure may be partially ameliorating the traits. That model is both kind and firm, demonstrates enormous respect for the basic nature of the child while simultaneously guiding the child towards respect of others.

Again this is <u>not</u> to blame parents for personality disorders. The traits are heritable; the disorders are not. Options in how to deal with the traits are not inherited. If there is a secure attachment and no history of drug or alcohol use within the family and no trauma, we can, as parents, help the traits become less troublesome both to our children as they grow into adults and to our families. Even with trauma and other above-mentioned factors, I have found that a parenting approach based on love facilitates healing and growth. My comments are based upon observation, not scientific research.

Whether you are a parent or other family member, this model is an attempt to help families identify behaviors that lie outside the channel. The goal is to remain inside the safety of the channel. Therefore behavior that is outside the channel (i.e., entitlement in an adolescent) can be guided back to the channel using the guiding force of that channel (i.e., belonging). When the issue is entitlement, it is incumbent upon family members to be clear and loving about what it takes to belong to a family. In other words, what work does the entitled person need to do so they can feel like they belong and participate within the family? You have already read many examples of entitlement, such as the girl who believed her family should have waited to have the birthday party but did not acknowledge her need to tell her family where she was going or when she might return.

When an adult child or spouse is screaming and blaming others, limits tell us how to respond to such dysregulation. Limits are the guiding force in the channel of protection. It is up to you to state that you cannot talk with the person who is dysregulated, that you are not leaving the relationship but you are leaving the conversation. Only you can protect yourself and disengage from a destructive barrage. Given your relationship, it is important to state when or under what circumstances you are willing to talk. I have heard mothers married to husbands with BPD instruct their children to disengage from their fathers when he was in a rage. All parties gained. He knew the behavior was not OK. His children learned it was OK to take care of themselves when adults are out of control.

The following diagram was introduced in my book, *The Journey of Parenting*. The model works for all relationships, not just parenting.

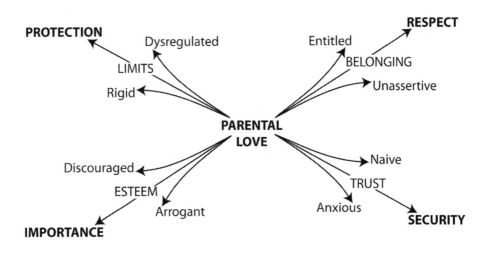

Security: As a parent works to build security, the dynamic that propels them down the channel is <u>trust</u>, which is based upon sameness and reliability. Too much trust over the course of a child's development leads to a child who is naïve; too little leads to a child who is anxious. Now if we add a very sensitive temperament and potential distortions of parent-child interactions, you must realize the child was born out of the channel, but your consistency and steadfastness helps the child regain equilibrium or head back toward the channel. Some children are born with the anxious genetic predisposition. Although I am speculating, clearly trust and learning about trustworthiness of others and eventually ourselves could only benefit such people. For a child, trust means you arrive on time to pick him up.

When dealing with an adult, security is also important. You must realize the measured amount you provide will help the other adult realize what you can and cannot do for them. The other adult must learn how to trust himself, not just you. An adult with a personality disorder recognizes he cannot trust himself to stay in control. He may justify his lack of control by saying someone else's behavior made him lose control, but that still means he cannot trust himself to stay in control.

Protection: Within the channel I designate as protection, the guiding principle is <u>limits</u>. When an adult dysregulates, it is important for the other adult to set limits on what she will and will not tolerate. Setting limits needs to be differentiated from abandonment. You can care for another and expect to have discussions, not yelling. You can care for another and yet not pay his bills or do his work. Remember that codependence disables your loved ones.

Importance: As we go down the channel of importance the progress is propelled by a sense of <u>true esteem</u>. The far shoal of making a child too important leads to arrogance. On the far shoal of too little importance, a child becomes discouraged. You will see examples later in this book where the mother valued her adult daughter too much. She paid her bills, fed her things she could not afford, and did not expect the daughter to contribute either work or money. This was not a valuing based on true esteem. True esteem would validate that the daughter was capable.

Respect: Finally, down the channel of respect, which is propelled by a sense of <u>belonging,</u> you have already seen many examples where a person with BPD required family members to respect her needs or concerns. Yet that same person seemed unaware she was not reciprocating respect. On the opposite shoal is the person who expects little or nothing from others and may be the overachiever victim Noel Larson describes. Parents teach their child about belonging by making sure she contributes to the family. Some parents have a tendency to not ask for any such contributions. A parent cannot instill a sense of belonging in a child by doing all her work for her. Her sense of belonging must come from her own actions.

Please keep in mind I am not blaming parents, but instead am pointing out the most extreme danger of going far out of the channel and the benefit of redirecting adults and children into the channel. In *The Journey of Parenting*, I give examples of children at various ages who are acting anxious, naïve, dysregulated, rigid, arrogant, discouraged, entitled, or unassertive. These behaviors are simply clues that they are out of the channel that provides a better pathway to adulthood. I also discuss how those very behaviors may be related to a conflict the parent is having. The conflict lies within the parent. The parent's desire to help a child become a competent, caring, and contributing adult, may be in direct conflict with a fear of their own (such as a parent's fear of conflict, fear of not being liked, or fear of their child not being happy).

Recognition and knowledge of this conflict allows the parent the opportunity to not react to their fear, but instead make a choice in parenting, which will lead them to their goal: a competent, caring, contributing adult. The choice is guided by considering what propels the parenting boat in that channel; that is, trust, limits, esteem, or belonging. Examples are: 1) If the child is dysregulated in their behavior or emotions, then limits help move them back within the channel, or 2) If the child is entitled, belonging and knowing what it takes to belong on both sides of a relationship guides the parent's choices. If you are a family member dealing with an adult with a personality disorder or a parent dealing with a child, the same guidelines apply. Observe the behavior and emotions. Decide upon which shoal the loved one is stuck. Then respond by choosing what you can do to help move the interaction back toward the center of the channel. This response is an act of love and should be done in a loving but clear manner.

Although I am not claiming to be a specialist in treating personality disorder, it is my hope to provide a point of connection between the loved one (i.e., a parent, sibling, child, spouse) and the family member with a personality disorder. The concept of validation is discussed in the book, *The High Conflict Couple: A Dialectical Behavior Therapy Guide to Finding Peace, Intimacy and Validation*, written by Marsha Linehan and Alan Fruzzetti. Validation is a point of connection and, as in parenting, must always begin with the goal of security first, then protection, then importance, and, finally, lessons in respect.

Once safety is established, there are limits to all relationships; esteem is based not on distortion and false praise and belonging is established by earning it. Along the channels, given what really happens in the life of someone with a personality disorder and the distortion lens the person wears, certain fears redirect his/her path out of the healthy part of the channel. For instance, if a person's issue is security, I suggest the fear that blocks the channel and causes misdirection is a fear of being wrong and/or wronged. For whatever reason, the person has an issue with trust of self and others. A person's fear or loss of control may have misdirected them off of the path to protection.

Nancy McWilliams, author of *Psychoanalytic Diagnosis, Second Edition: Understanding Personality Structure in the Clinical Process,* states that people with ASPD have need for omnipotent control. The path to importance is misdirected by a fear of invisibility and/or meaninglessness. Arrogant people actually suffer from a lack of self-importance. Finally, the path to respect is blocked by a fear of abandonment. Without a sense of belonging we all feel abandoned. How is a person with BPD or ASPD to know he set up his own abandonment when he does not know what it takes to belong?

It may help family members understand their family member with BPD or ASPD by understanding the fears that block the path. However, understanding is different than justifying or accepting the behaviors within the family. *Feeling* abandoned and *being* abandoned are different. Just because we feel it, does not make it so. The SOS person in her constant blaming, criticizing, and punishing her family members often unintentionally sets up abandonment. Fear begets that which we are afraid of. It can become a self-fulfilling prophecy.

The question a family member faces in dealing with another member with a personality disorder is: How do I respond to this behavior in a way that tries to be my best self? You cannot change your family member. You can only change yourself. Changing yourself does not mean you allow the person to emotionally or physically manipulate you. You need to respond in a respectful way so you walk away with your respect intact. It may mean you do not talk to the SOS but write them a short note. Another option is to walk away from the conversation, designating another time to talk when all parties are calm. You may even have to set certain rules that, if violated, will mean you will leave the relationship. All this must be done in a tone that is firm but loving. Do not dwell on the SOS's behavior, simply what you can do to move towards your wish for a more respectful relationship.

The model below represents the fears that lie upon the path to security, protection, importance, and respect.

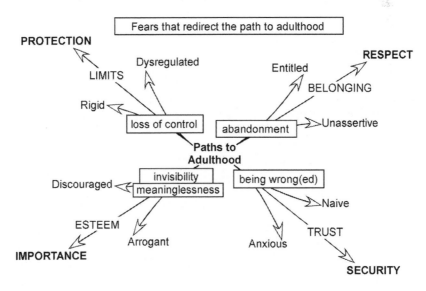

These fears may block an SOS person's path. However, you cannot be the therapist. The SOS individual has to *want* to change. Only the SOS person can change his behavior. You, as a family member, may wish or hope for a change, but only he can do the work of change. He is an adult.

In the following chapters, you will learn practical ways of dealing with an SOS loved one. These chapters are focused on the dynamics of being in a relationship with someone with BPD or ASPD, whether it be a spouse, a parent, a sibling, or an adult child.

TALES FROM THE TRENCHES

CHAPTER FOUR

A Parent with BPD or ASPD

A Poem by a 4th grade girl with a mom with BPD:

You broke me
not in half,
not in pieces.
You did not chip me.
You did not fracture me.
You broke my heart.
But slowly,
oh ever so slowly,
my heart is healing.
I do not like you.
I do not love you.
I absolutely adore you.
You are my one and only mom.
Words cannot describe how much I feel for you.
I love you.
Please remember that.

Growing up with a parent with a personality disorder is like trying to grow up while walking upon a field of ice on the top of a quake line. There are frequent earthquakes ranging from 1.5 to 8.5 on the Richter scale.

Every day or week a new quake occurs while at the same time the child tries to find balance on the ice. In retrospect, some of the more difficult times, expressed to me by the adult children, have to do with the process of learning that they cannot believe what the parent tells them. They remember so many times when they felt crazy because they wished they knew who to believe: dad or mom, dad or aunt, grandma or mom.

This difficulty in discerning truth is combined with a great loyalty bind to the parent. These children have witnessed what happens to the people who get on their parent's bad side or are disloyal. That person is shunned or abandoned. The children feel guilty for even knowing what they know: that their parent is unreliable and lies. Figuring out that they have a parent who lies takes a long time, especially given that SOS parents often tell their child "I will never lie to you."

It seems the difficulties encountered have to do with the following categories:

- the parent's creation of drama and their need to be the center of attention;
- the parent's lack of ability to take into account their child's perspective or development;
- the parent's need to look good to the child;
- the parent's need to be seen as a victim, which leads to splitting the family;
- the parent's need for absolute loyalty and their inability to sustain the work or discipline of life.

What follows are the stories of Paul and Mary. Paul grew up with a father with ASPD; Mary grew up with a mother with BPD. I have written these stories from the first-person perspective and have combined different people's stories so you, the reader, can feel like you are listening to Paul or Mary speaking.

A. Paul's Story as a Seventeen-Year-Old

What I remember most in my elementary years were my father's women. There were always women. Some would last two or three years.

Then came the woman who worked as a stripper when I was in 4th grade. She told both my sister, who was in 2nd grade, and me all about her breast enlargements and about her sexual exploits. I remember visiting my dad, but it seemed the women always made the rules. Maybe I'm wrong about that. He used to argue a lot with some of them.

Oh, I forgot to mention he moved a lot. Sometimes he lived with the women; sometimes not. I hated visitation weekends. One time when I was in 4th grade he moved into a house with white carpet and white furniture. My sister and I were not even allowed in half of that house. We might have messed it up.

Mom hated sending us to Dad's, but the judge had ordered his visitation. Mom said she didn't trust him to take care of us. Dad was often fun if he was around, but he always favored my sister. She got whatever she wanted. Mostly, I just got confused.

He always had big plans: he was going to marry this woman, he was going to buy me a Moped, he was going to get us another house... Sometimes he did, sometimes he didn't. He always seemed to want to do things that Mom wouldn't or couldn't do.

One time he promised us a dog. We had a dog while he lived with Cherie. But the dog stayed with her when they broke up, so there went the dog.

I remember seeing Dr. Linda when I was ten. She said it seemed to her my life was like a soap opera on television, but someone had forgotten to give me a remote control. I really wanted one too. I didn't like my Dad or the visits. There was just too much drama.

My dad was often mad at my mom. He used to say she was just too uptight. He let me ride a motorcycle with him when I was eight and I didn't have a helmet. Boy, was Mom upset when she found out. We didn't have bedtimes at his house. She didn't like that at all. He told us she had asked for the divorce and that he never wanted it. He often told us he didn't have any money but I didn't understand; he always seemed to spend a lot of it. He bought me a four-wheeler when I was ten. But then he said he had to store it when he moved when I was eleven. I never saw it again.

Mom was particularly worried whenever he drove us places. Much later, when I was in my teens, I found out Dad didn't have insurance on his car.

He always had a car, but the car didn't have in-state license plates. By the time I was a teen, Dad worked in a state other than the one in which we lived. Mom said that made it easy for him to not pay income tax. By that time Mom had shared that we had to be careful with our money. It seems my Dad had never paid child support.

I wondered why my Dad worked in another state when his brother, my uncle, did the same work in our state. When I was fourteen, I asked my uncle why he didn't work with my dad. My uncle hemmed and hawed and finally told me the story. It seems they had all worked together when I was little. Dad, according to Uncle Gary, had embezzled several hundred thousand dollars from the company. My uncle, instead of charging Dad legally, made him pay back what he could. Now Uncle Gary just doesn't work with my dad. I also remembered I hadn't seen much of that side of the family since I was six. Dad had always told me it was because they took Mom's side in the divorce.

One of the reasons I hated visiting Dad was I often felt like I had to take care of my sister. Now don't get me wrong, I love my sister. But with his changes in women and house I often had the job of keeping her in line. Dad treated her like a little princess, but when he was gone he assumed I'd take care of her. When you're only eight that becomes tiresome. The good times with Dad seemed to be when there wasn't a woman around. Dad would let us stay up late, eat what we wanted, and pretty much watch whatever we wanted on television.

The real problem for me began when I was about fifteen. My mom and I started arguing a lot. She did seem awfully controlling to me. She had a curfew for me. Mom found out I was drinking with my friends when I was sixteen and grounded me from the car she bought for my use. It was miserable, so I headed to my Dad's. He'd just bought my sister a horse so I figured he owed me. He bought me a new car so I just started living with him. Given that he worked out of state Monday through Friday, I was on my own. It was kind of like being his roommate. No rules, just keep the place clean while he was gone. I had friends over and we hung out. All went well until I got a DUI. Dad went ballistic.

At that point I went back to Mom, who was so relieved to have me back she took me in. I told her I would follow her rules: be in by midnight and not drink. She sure had a thing about laws. Mom said midnight was the legal curfew for our city and I was an underage drinker. She said she was worried because Dad wasn't a good role model on obeying the rules. But I knew from what Dad had said that her side of the family was just way too uptight. I knew no one followed the curfew laws and all my friends drank. So after a while I began to ignore her rules again. She just turned into a bitch and I just stayed gone most of the time.

I was thinking about heading back to Dad's to live. But then I had another problem: another DUI. This time they said I'd have to spend time in juvie since I'd gotten two in a year and was underage. Mom came forward and offered to pay for a stint in rehab. The judge said OK but only after a week in jail. Dad was nowhere to be found. He said he was working out of state. Mom told me that he couldn't go near a court given all the laws he was evading. The courts then ordered me to live with Mom. I was mad at the judge. I'm no one's property. Who was he to tell me where to live?

B. Mary's Story

My sister and I went to live with Grandma and Grandpa (Dad's Mom and Dad) when I was five. My Mama lived with us there the first nine months. Then my Mama's parents bought her a house four blocks away from Grandma and Grandpa. We were confused why we didn't live with Mama. They told us she had a night job, and it was better on school days that we stayed with them since Mama was gone all night and was tired all day. We cried, we missed our Mama, but we went to her house on the weekends.

Let's start at the beginning. Mama left Dad when I was about three. She said he used drugs and we had to leave to be safe. She took my sister, little Kiki, and me to live with her mom (Maman) and Boppa. We lived there almost a year but Boppa was sick. Maman said it was too hard for him to have little children around.

From there we moved to Grandma's and Grandpa's house. They lived a long way away from everybody else we knew. We were scared at first. Mama said we really had to behave this time. That was confusing to me because I thought I was behaving. I was even working hard to teach Kiki to behave.

She was younger and I tried to keep her in line. As it was, I had always tried to help Mama. When she didn't feel well, I'd play with Kiki. I was the big one. I'd figured out how to get us food and I'd even figured out how to change Kiki's diaper. Sometimes I am responsible for taking care of Mama when she feels bad. She has felt bad a lot since we left Daddy.

When my sister is sick and we are at Mama's for the weekend, I sometimes don't go to church with Grandma and Grandpa. I think it's best to stay and take care of Kiki even though I really like church. I feel safe at church. Grandma often says that I don't have to stay to take care of Kiki. She thinks it's too big a job for me. Once Dr. Linda told me grown-ups take care of children; it's not the child's job to take care of grown-ups. That makes sense, but they don't have my Mama and I just don't want to disappoint her.

Sometimes she disappoints me though. She sometimes doesn't come to my choir performances. Mama always says something came up, but I get sad anyway. The other day when we were about to leave for a play I was in at school, Mama called and asked me if I wanted to go with her for an ice cream cone. I explained I had to go to school for the play that I had already told her about. She came to the play, which I thought was great. When she doesn't show up I just keep searching for her in the audience.

Mama sometimes shows up at our extended daycare after school. She comes to give us hugs and kisses. I finally had to ask her not to come anymore. When she showed up, Kiki and I would want to leave with her and go home. Kiki always cried because she would leave without us. I didn't like Kiki crying.

Mama treats us like little grown-ups. She told me and Kiki all about French kissing, sex, getting her tubes tied so she couldn't have any more babies, and drugs. She tells us not to tell our Grandma since Grandma will get mad at her. Kiki was talking at kindergarten about sex and French kissing. She's not as good at keeping secrets as me. The teacher called Grandma. Grandma wasn't mad, but she did say what we were talking about was really for older children. She asked Kiki not to talk about it with her friends. She said it was for the other parents to explain to their own children.

Mama makes the rules and seems to get mad at Grandma and Grandpa if they don't follow them. It's confusing. She says "television rots your brains" and told our Grandparents we shouldn't be allowed to watch. Grandma and Grandpa had just let us watch one program before we went to school. Now we can't. That stinks. But when we are at Mama's sometimes we watch lots and lots of TV.

Last Halloween Mama came over to Grandma's and took home with her half of the candy we'd collected. We never saw it again. She told Grandma we should not be allowed to have so much sugar. I know she ate it. She didn't have any right to it, but I can't tell her. She keeps telling me I'm too fat. She says I stink because my body is changing. I will take a bath and put on my Dove crème Grandma bought me. She still says I stink.

I walk to school each day. So do most kids in my neighborhood. It's about six blocks. Mama told me all about kidnappers and people who strap bombs to themselves to blow up schools and places. I got really scared. Grandma told me that kidnappers and bomb people are very unusual. The people with the bombs are mostly halfway across the world from us. The kidnappings don't happen much and have not occurred in our neighborhood. We decided it was best if I walked with a friend. Mama said that wasn't enough. She bought me a cell phone. Grandma thought I was too young for a cell phone. I was only eight. Oh and I lost it three weeks later. Mama got really mad at me.

Mama says my dad is not a good man. She says he does drugs. He forgets my birthday, Christmas, and we rarely hear from him. That's OK though. Last birthday I got lots of presents from other people. Grandma and Grandpa bought me some games and a bicycle I wanted. Maman, my Mama's mom bought me an iPod, earrings, and some DVDs rated PG-13. Grandma and Grandpa won't let me watch the DVDs because I'm only nine, not thirteen. I haven't really got pierced ears, but I like the earrings. Boppa sent me a chemistry set. It says it's meant for age thirteen and above. He was a chemist at a big company. Grandma and Grandpa put it away for later. They said we could all read the directions and try to do it together since I really don't understand how to use it.

Last month Mama said she was going to get a dog. We went shopping and she asked the sales person lots of questions. I thought we were all set, but then she said I'd have to keep the dog at Grandma's house. She didn't think she could take care of the dog while I was at Grandma's house during the school week. She said I'd have to ask Grandma and Grandpa if I could keep the dog all week at their house. I asked, but they feel like they are busy enough with Sis and me.

Shortly after we went to live with Grandma and Grandpa we met Dr. Linda. They thought she could help us. We were sad about Mom's not living with us and Kiki was having trouble at school.

C. Helping Paul and Mary

Paul and Mary are at various stages of life and insight. Mary is confused by her Mama, loves her, protects her, and believes what she says. Mary is often caught in Mama's dramas. Mama promises a dog and then makes Grandma and Grandpa the bad guys for her not buying one, thereby triangulating the children. She says they can get a dog but only if the grandparents do all the work. By living with Grandma and Grandpa, Mary gets a different perspective, she gets boundaries, she gets to be respected in an age-appropriate way as a child. Grandma and Grandpa work very hard not to judge her Mama and not say anything to place Mary and Kiki in the middle between Mama and them. This is not an easy task. Grandma often feels like she is undoing the damage Mama does to Mary and Kiki on the weekends. Grandma walks a fine line; she knows if she does not, Mama could take the children and leave. She also knows Mama is not capable of taking care of her own children. Since Grandma and Grandpa have had the children in their house, Mama has lost her job two times. Even when Mama isn't working, she doesn't see the children during the week. Often she asks Grandma and Grandpa to keep them on Saturday nights too. Yet when Grandma and Grandpa need help they have to call upon friends. Mama says it's hard for her to make a commitment. Dad lives in another state, still seems to be using drugs, and is rarely in contact with his parents.

As you read Mary's story of being a child of a parent with BPD you see how things don't make sense. There are no routines at Mom's house. Mom is a hoarder and the house is a mess. There are glimpses that Mom grew up with parents who give gifts with little knowledge of the age, developmental appropriateness, or interests of the granddaughters. They pay for their daughter's life with little expectation of what the daughter needs to do in return. The grandparents who are raising the grandchildren are given all the responsibility of daily care with little authority in decision-making outside of their own home.

When Mary and Kiki play in my office they clearly believe the only reason they do not live with Mama is her job. Kiki longs for the time they can live with Mama. Now that Mary is older she has begun to realize not all of what Mama says is true. Mary even corrected Kiki once when Kiki told me they were all going on a big vacation this summer. Mary simply said, "Not everything Mom says is true."

Because little minds are concrete operational in their thinking, they think in terms of all or nothing, good or bad. It is too difficult for them to comprehend at this point that Mama may love them but not have the ability to follow through with that love. Love to children has to do with action and consistency and follow-through. Love is the ability to make the child's needs more important than your own. These are not strengths for a parent with BPD.

At this point in her life, Mary cannot understand mental illness. After all, her Mama looks healthy much of the time. As she grows older, eventually Grandma or I will explain to her what her Mama's problem is. However, this may violate Mom's no-talk rule and could be difficult to do without Mom going into a rage and trying to remove the children from either Grandma's care or my care.

Right now Mary is simply and slowly figuring out there is a problem. Why doesn't she live with Mama? How come Mama doesn't come to events that are important to her? How come Mama says things that are different when she talks to Grandma? "Mama says she loves me but she says I stink." "Mama doesn't come to choir concerts, and she doesn't take me to the doctor." "What does this mean?" she wonders. At this point Mary needs a helping witness, someone who can reiterate what she sees or experiences. In that way Mary can feel less crazy.

The good news is that she and Kiki have very dedicated grandparents. They serve as role models of self-discipline and emotional regulation. By their actions they will mentor another way of being and thinking in their granddaughters. They consistently place their grandchildren's needs above their own needs to express their problems with Mama. They work to try to get both girls time with their Mama. In that way the girls will learn about their Mama, who she is and what she has to offer, on their own. They step out of the game of splitting the girls' heart in two by not making them choose who is the "good" one.

Children learn the differences between the people who love them over time, but unfortunately, it may take a long time. They may be in their twenties before they are old enough and secure enough to say "I love my Mama but she lies or she distorts, she may not be here, she tries to turn me against others," etc.

Paul is in a different kind of danger. Although Mom has raised him to self-regulate, his adolescent hormones push him towards dysregulation. This is a time when many young people believe they are as smart as the adults in their lives. By their very nature, adolescents are narcissistic or self-involved and loathe rules or the responsibilities that come with privileges.

In essence, Dad is behaving like a permanent adolescent. Dad's idea of not following society's laws is very appealing. Dad no longer seems an ogre, but instead an avenue to freedom for Paul, to have what he wants with few responsibilities. Dad's thinking is appealing: "If Dad can drive without insurance, so can I. My problem is really that Mom is a bully, too controlling. I don't have to think about my part in the arguments with Mom." Adolescence is a dangerous time to have an option of living with a parent with a personality disorder. It allows Paul to grow but without boundaries and often without compassion. It allows Paul the privileges of adulthood without the responsibilities.

The approach to helping Paul is different from that with Mary. With Mary I remain a helping witness to her world. Over time I help her know what she only suspects. I role model another way of connecting. With Paul I am a sane, neutral voice. I have known Paul a long time. He knows I am connected to him and only want the best for him. With him I question his part in his story. I cannot let him continue to blame other people for his choices. I serve as a sounding board but also as another adult who cares about Paul and his future. I come to the table with over thirty-five years of experience and have encountered many families and different rules in families. Paul and I discuss boundaries and laws, the role they play in society, and in our personal relationship. I challenge him about how he is now using Dad to run from Mom, and also to run from the basic respect and responsibility of any relationship. I challenge him to be better. I challenge him to be a male who obeys laws.

The most difficult part for the people who are attached to a child of an ASPD or BPD is helping them to discern how to live a healthy life. As a grandparent, a mother, a dad, a therapist, somehow you have to counterbalance a destructive role model. A parent who models self absorption, who gains attention through pain or sickness, who lies and who break rules, is powerful and seductive. It is difficult—for those of us who are trying to provide another option—to discern what the source is when we see these same behaviors in a child. Is the child simply modeling what they have observed in their parent? Parents and grandparents worry if some genetic door is opening to another family member being ill. My contention is genetics are not the issue. What really matters is trying to get this child to see another course; another option that will lead them to recognize love when offered. It is my belief that all children will have the best chance at happiness if they become competent, caring, and contributing adults. We, as their caregivers must keep our eye on those goals and not let our fears take over and drive our caregiving ship. It is our job to try to steer the child back towards the middle of the channel.

Depending on the age of the child, the best I can do as therapist is to be a safe place. A safe place is where the child can express their world view or what they have learned about the world and have their reality affirmed that certain behaviors hurt, confuse, frustrate, or sadden them. My office is a safe place where no one is put down, not their mother, their father, their grandmother, or the bully at school. Instead, as they play, they can learn how to identify their feelings, learn it is not their fault that others do these things that hurt them and problem-solve ways to handle situations so they don't have to be repeatedly hurt.

This role is what we as therapists often refer to as a helping witness. It is not my role to change the parent. If I were to enter that role it would conflict with my role of helping the child. As a helper to their child, I will help the parent understand the needs of their child. However, given the history of people with ASPD or BPD firing therapists, I walk a fine line trying not to get fired. If that were to happen, it would set up one more loss for the child. I often serve as another voice, speaking on behalf of the child to the parent's therapist. In that way their therapist gains another perspective about damage to the loved ones their client cannot see and may not wish to acknowledge in their own therapy.

As the child ages into adolescence, if the child is ready to breach the loyalty divide the parent set up, I can acknowledge what the adolescent knows about their parent by naming it. I can discuss what they have experienced in the context of a mental illness. In no way do I ever question the fact that the parent loves their child. However, I can help the adolescent learn that because of the personality disorder the parent cannot display that love in the way the child wishes, or deserves, or needs. It is helpful for the adolescent to begin to discern how their parent does care and yet may not be able to be there for them in the ways they wish or they need as they continue to grow into adulthood.

D. Children of a Parent with Personality Disorder: How They Look

I am often asked to describe the children of SOS parents. Alone, each pattern might not indicate that the parent has a personality disorder. But cumulatively, I see definite correlations.

I have several games in my office that I use in my work with children. Children who have one or more parents with a personality disorder almost always ask to play a game called "Mind Your Manners." It is an old game in which a player moves forward or backwards depending upon manners. The manners cards vary from being as simple as rewarding a child for not placing their elbows on the table, to saying "please" and "thank you," or waiting for the other people to get off an elevator before getting on. The cards give negative points for behaviors like interrupting a parent while she is on the telephone or not listening to the teacher.

It is important for the child of a parent with a borderline personality disorder to learn the rules. Often the child's life has been chaotic. Emotional outbursts by the parent have been random. The child believes if he could understand the rules and follow them his parent would be happy, not angry.

But the rules keep changing. The child wants to learn manners in hopes of gaining a feeling of belonging. He also hopes that in following the rules he might not experience as much emotional dysregulation from the parent.

Another game the children play is my "Feelings" card game. It is a game that has pictures of people's facial expressions, which represent certain emotions. The child or I mimic the facial expression in an attempt to learn what emotion is being expressed. Children of an SOS parent often do not understand feelings, especially their own. There has only been room for the parent's emotion within the home. The child has little experience in identifying her own emotions.

Often the child has been isolated from other adults and family members. The parent with ASPD isolates the child through a constant conversation about how others are untrustworthy. This can be open or very subtle, implying that they, like the dad, would never do what Mom does. This isolation helps in the control of the child's world view. The parent with BPD does this process as well but usually in a more triangulating manner. The effect is the same: resulting in a child who does not trust other adults—be it their grandparent, their teacher, or me.

In addition to the games in my office, I also have sand trays. The child places characters, buildings, and other features in these trays to create worlds in the sand. These worlds reflect how they see the world in which they live. The child of a parent with ASPD or BPD typically creates worlds in which there are no adults because they do not trust them. One child in the middle of a very nasty divorce recently built a home for her and her sister. She then built two other houses, one for her mom and one for her dad, but they were not allowed to visit the children's home. She then built a playground next to the children's house where I could come and visit.

Children are confused by the very different realities they face when they are with Mom versus Dad. Young children are very concrete. People are right or wrong. They tell the truth or they lie. Therefore they trust no one after a while or they cling to one parent's reality. When they are old enough to question their own experience versus the reality they have been given, they get angry at the lies they have been told.

The child of a parent with ASPD has certain presentations that differ from the child with a parent with BPD. Sons may be especially vulnerable to a father with ASPD. By watching his dad, he may learn that rules do not apply to him. Some of my clients, who have fathers with ASPD, try to justify to me that lies are OK. I have heard it isn't a lie to the parent without ASPD if the child doesn't talk about what he has done. He sincerely believe lies are fine. For instance, he may be asked not to talk to Mom about activities Dad allows in his house, even if those activities are unsafe. When such children play in my office they often change the rules of play in mid-game. Winning is all-important. Some of the children exhibit arrogance, believing they know everything about everything just as Dad role models arrogance at home. Recently, one boy was looking at keys to my office. When he saw one that said "Do not duplicate," he immediately said, "Let's make a copy."

What these children long for is a parent who is secure and consistent in their world. They want each parent to never put down the other parent, because the parent recognizes that such behavior only hurts the child. Looking long term, all parents should recognize that saying bad things about the other parent will eventually destroy the relationship with their own child.

Around such children, adult behavior needs to be consistent and non-judgmental. The adult accepts the right of every child to love both their parents even if one or both have a mental illness. That adult could be a grandparent, an aunt, an uncle, or a therapist. The child often believes the parent with BPD or ASPD, so it is critical that steadfastness helps them see you are a safe person. In the cases where the child has rejected one parent due to being influenced by the parent with BPD or ASPD, the child can potentially return to a more even balance. It takes the rejected parent reaching out with notes, with memories, with the steadfast message of "I love you forever; I love you always." That, along with the rejected parent's steadfast rejection to play the "let's put each other down" game, serves as a lighthouse of safety for the child as he begins to wake up and come out of the trance in which he has lived.

In the meantime, there are parenting coaches who can help along the way. There are programs, like Bill Eddy's High Conflict Institute, to coach parents in how to speak to their child, which can help. However, keep in mind parents with BPD and ASPD truly believe they are doing nothing wrong, therefore, they may not be open to help or to change.

E. Conclusion:

As any child grows into adulthood, he will seek approval from his parent. I wrote the following poem in a Dr. Seuss-style, depicting what I saw happening between a "50 something" son and his father who had borderline traits.

The Tale of Chester McChesney

Chester McChesney was a brilliant man.
He'd made millions in ventures throughout all the land.
He was generous and giving to lots of good causes.
Through hard work and fame he made gains not losses.

Fester McChesney was Chester's old father
Chester gave to his dad and said "It's no bother."
He bought many presents including a house.
None of them made Fester happy—the louse.

Ole Fester would grumble.
Ole Fester would mumble.
Things always were wrong with what Chester did.
Chester never felt any love from the old squid.

Chester couldn't make Fester happy or proud.
Fester'd rant about what was wrong and be loud.
The grander Chester got with his gifts.
The more that Fester got really miffed.

Said Chester to Fester "Enough is enough.
I can't make you happy it's just way too tough."
I know I'm a good son said a voice in his head.
I'll listen to it, so I won't want you dead.

One of the most difficult things an adult child of a personality disordered parent has to learn is to quit reacting to either the verbal, or sometimes nonverbal, expressions of that parent. The parent has become an expert at manipulating the people around them to get their own SOS needs met. One lesson the adult child needs to learn is best told as a Marine statement in Tanya Huff's *The Truth of Valor*, "No one ever bled out as the result of a pissy expression." Translated, this means the adult child needs to quit reacting to the verbal and nonverbal expressions as if they are bullets. Frequently, they feel as if they are mortally wounded as a result of the exchange with the parent. The adult child must take their power back and accept these expressions as just being pissy. They need to make a decision to listen to the truth of the issue and set boundaries about how often and for how long they can be with their parent if that parent continues to make such comments.

When coparenting with someone with BPD or ASPD you must become a Rock of Gibraltar for the child. Your consistency and integrity in not speaking poorly of the SOS parent will allow the child to grow and learn from her own experiences with her SOS parent. Your ability to set healthy limits for her and the SOS parent will provide a guide for how she might speak up and protect herself as she grows.

CHAPTER FIVE

A Sibling with BPD or ASPD

Powerlessness is the most difficult aspect of dealing with any family member who has a personality disorder. You cannot change them. In the case of the sibling, you cannot change the ways your parents enable or disable the family member with a personality disorder. It is important to realize the only person you can change is *you*. You have to step out of a role in which you were placed as a child. It will destroy you if you remain disconnected from yourself, have no needs, and constantly work hard for your sibling's, or potentially your parents', approval.

Peter's story reveals a very dysfunctional family in which Peter's sister, Elaina, has BPD. Peter had to learn many skills as a child to survive. Then he had to unlearn those dysfunctional skills as an adult. Peter had to work hard in the family he created with his wife and children to learn a more connected way of being a family. It has taken years. There have been steps forward and steps backward.

He and his wife continue to find connection while dealing with a family of origin in which there is a lifetime of denial and disconnection. Peter has learned to stay present to the people he loves. Fortunately for Peter, he had some mentors. In his childhood and early marriage he had a very loving grandmother and grandfather. The grandmother listened while he spoke—she connected.

Peter's wife has worked hard to listen. It has taken Peter much work to learn to listen to himself and to those he loves. He has had to struggle with his dislike of conflict and his own tendencies toward addiction.

Sylvia is another example of a sibling to someone with ASPD. As in the case with Peter, the family denial is recognizable. In this example there are very different ways family members handle the problem—a brother who has disconnected and a sister who attempts for a period of time to be an overachiever victim.

The common thread here is that both Peter and Sylvia feel powerless. Both have grown up without the ability to take care of themselves. Each of them thought their experience was normal up to a point, and then challenged their own denial system. Both siblings have been silently asked to be invisible, to not have needs, and/or to over-function for their parents. Peter and Sylvia have both had to learn how to set healthy boundaries for themselves.

A. Peter's Story

I grew up in the fifties in what would eventually be an upper middle class family. My mom was a stay-at-home mother. My father eventually became a CEO of a small business. I had one sister, Elaina, who was born six years after me.

As I grew up, my father rarely had time for me. I spent lots of time in my room building models and other projects. Dad was either at work or playing golf. Golf to him was his love and also the way he got work through the good-old-boy system. Once in a while he would play golf with me but mostly he was gone. Later I realized "gone" also meant drinking. Much later I realized that, although my father functioned at work, much of the rest of the time he was drinking. At our home Mom would just say, "Dad's not feeling well," or "He's under the weather." Not identifying his alcoholism meant I assumed for many years he didn't like me because I was smart, and not athletic, like he had been as a boy.

My mom was devoted to my sister after she was born. My mother always patted her on her back as she went to sleep at night. Elaina was different. I didn't realize how different until I was much older. She was the baby and was always treated that way. She was the girl, which meant she was supposed to be pretty and not much else was expected of her.

Later, a few years after college, I got married. Elaina was a senior in high school. My wife wanted to get to know my sister. She invited Elaina and her boyfriend to dinner. My wife cooked for several hours with the expectation that we would have a nice evening. She wanted to play games or cards with them. Elaina came over with Scott, ate, and then immediately left our apartment, saying she and Scott had plans.

I knew my wife was disappointed, but I thought maybe I had forgotten to tell Elaina that we were planning to have some fun that evening. My wife said it was weird that Elaina had not even offered to help with the dishes or anything. She had stayed to eat and then left with her boyfriend like my wife was our mother.

The next year my mom asked if we could come to dinner the night of my wife's birthday to celebrate. We went. My father had picked up Elaina from her college dorm in our city to join us for dinner. All through dinner my parents catered to Elaina, who was obviously sulking about something. It was as if my wife and I weren't there. After dinner, my wife suggested she and I go on a walk to give the three of them time to settle their differences. We excused ourselves and left for a walk before dessert.

My wife was upset. She said she knew my mother's intentions had been good, but this wasn't a good way to spend her birthday. We went back for dessert and a present, thanked them, and left. The tension in the house made it difficult to stay.

These incidents kept happening. It seemed when the whole family gathered, Elaina would sulk or pout, and my folks would try to cajole her out of it. When one of her boyfriends would join us she would be in a better mood. However, my wife noticed that if a family picture was taken, Elaina would tell my wife she couldn't be in it, and my mother wouldn't object. If Elaina's boyfriend was included then my mother said it was okay for my wife to be in the picture. My wife didn't like being treated the same as a boyfriend. No matter what, there seemed to be tension anytime my family gathered.

We kept trying to make peace with my sister. Once, when we were visited by a cousin named Anna who was Elaina's age, we invited Elaina to travel with us to show Anna Washington, DC.

Elaina came along but made the three of us miserable. Most of the time she wouldn't speak to my wife. She seemed mad at everything. After our first day on the road, we stopped late. We took the last two rooms at a hotel. There was only one double bed in the room Elaina and Anna shared. Unbeknownst to us, Elaina slept on the floor and was mad at my wife the rest of the trip. When we got up, Elaina took an hour primping while we all waited. I asked her to hurry it along but that only made her madder. Obviously, that was the end of ever inviting her to do nice things with us. She never even said thank you for the trip. Elaina went back to my parents' home where she was living at the time, and they then seemed to be mad at us too.

Over a ten-year period Elaina sometimes lived at home with our parents and sometimes in apartments for which I believe my dad paid. She was in college, but not the one she started at. For two years she had a part-time job, which I thought might have helped her become more independent. I was not clear how much money my dad gave her, but it seemed like a lot. They didn't talk about that. I did know that if her car broke she always asked daddy to arrange for and pay for the repair.

At one point, she had an apartment near us. Once in a while we would bump into her at the local grocery store. We would always try to be pleasant. On one occasion, my wife saw her and, having heard that Elaina's cat had died the month before, approached her to tell her she was sorry about the loss of her cat. Elaina replied, "You didn't even send me a card. I got cards from people who really care. Don't you get it? This is the same as if one of your children had died." My wife came home infuriated at her comparison of her cat to our children. My wife also pointed out that when her mother died two years before, Elaina had said nothing nor had she sent a card.

Despite all these incidents, when Elaina fell on the ice a year later, I was the first person she called. I picked her up, took her to the emergency room, and waited. She needed surgery and was going to be in the hospital a few days. My wife and I went to her house the next few days, got her things for her, fed her cat, etc., until she got out of the hospital. She then went to our parents to live for a period since she was on crutches. Although I was completely there for her, she did not say thank you or act in any way different to my wife or me after the crisis.

Now you may be wondering why I didn't ask my family to go to a therapist. I did, repeatedly. They wouldn't go. After the fall, Elaina went back to live with our parents again. Finally, she agreed to seek therapy. At the prompting of her therapist, the immediate family gathered, again excluding my wife. The focus then was upon how Elaina had been date raped at nineteen. I felt terrible for her, but this didn't explain her rudeness and my parents' denial about how she acted within the family. The therapy never got to those issues. After this, Elaina continued in therapy. In fact, she's still in therapy thirty years later. However, as my therapist explains, she makes sure that she controls what information her therapist hears. I am not invited.

Finally, nine years after she began college my parents told us she was graduating. We were not invited. She was also supposed to be getting married the next weekend. We were not invited to the wedding. My parents said it was a small civil ceremony with only immediate family. I always thought brothers were immediate family. Dad said she wanted money more than a wedding. She was going to move to another state where her new husband had been offered a job.

Before the move, I got a letter from her demanding the crib we had used for our two children and the children's table our youngest (who was four) still played at. The crib and table had originally belonged to my parents and both Elaina and I had used it as children. In the letter she stated she needed these items now in case she was to become pregnant. I called my mother and told her about the letter. Mom replied, "Elaina just gets things in her head. If I were you I would just give it to her."

The problem was we had loaned the crib to our dear friend who had just had her baby one week before. So I talked with my wife. We settled on giving Elaina our child's table and offered to ship the crib before she would give birth if she became pregnant. To this day my youngest thinks of her aunt as the adult who took her table away. She had no other reference for her as she had rarely seen her.

When our youngest was six our family was attending a cousin's wedding; Grandma and Grandpa were at the wedding. Our daughter asked why Grandpa and Grandma weren't sitting with us. And who was it that they were sitting with? It was Aunt Elaina, whom she didn't know or recognize. It hurt to see my family so split.

After Elaina married, she lived with her husband in another state for about the next nine years. I seldom saw her. My parents would visit her once or twice a year and she would come home once in a while. My parents didn't tell me when she visited, or how often they visited her. It was like my parents had two separate families. Once in a while, when they were worried, something would slip. I know Elaina was hospitalized two or three times. I found it odd that Mom didn't go see her when she was in the hospital. Mom seemed to be in constant touch with Elaina's husband, and, according to Mom, he had told her not to come.

There seemed to be many secrets about my sister. Toward the end of her marriage, my parents would only say his family was being mean to her. During this time she had a huge car accident that involved some legal problems. I always suspected she had been driving while overmedicated. While the divorce and her legal issues were being settled, Elaina moved back in with my parents. When living with them I witnessed how often she misused her medications. She had a problem taking more of her medicines than could possibly be prescribed. Elaina frequently slurred her words at family gatherings when she chose to attend one.

Once the divorce was final, she got an apartment in our state. Supposedly, her income was the alimony based on the divorce settlement. She took classes again and after two to three years tried to hold a job. It lasted two months. Elaina said they did not teach her how to do the job so she quit. But who knows, my guess was that she was fired. As the alimony was running out, she again moved back to Mom and Dad's house.

Once she came back to my parents' home this time, things seemed to continually get worse. My wife always cooked the holiday meals. On Christmas day we would get calls saying my parents and Elaina wouldn't be able to make dinner because Elaina wasn't feeling well. That became my mother's way of saying Elaina was overmedicated once again. Worse yet, sometimes they would let her drive them to our house when clearly she shouldn't have been driving; Elaina would be overmedicated and could hardly speak. I spoke to them about it out of concern, but they got upset with me.

It seemed to do no good. I asked them to go to therapy. They declined saying Elaina went to therapy and it really didn't help. At my parents' home, Elaina lived in a two-bedroom suite (my old bedroom and hers). She continued to live a life of luxury with a private phone line. She kept her hair colored and had nice-looking clothes. By this time, Elaina had no income other than my parents' gifts to her, and she had no motivation to work.

Several times I went out alone to visit with my parents and express my concern about them as well as what would happen to Elaina if something happened to them. They started dreading my visits with them and would say, "We are not going to have one of our talks, are we?"

In the early years of Elaina's final return, Mom and Dad would try to go on vacation. Twice she called them back early from their trip. They returned fearful for her safety. Although no one actually said so, it seemed obvious she threatened suicide. Finally, Mom and Dad just gave up. The three of them went everywhere together. They would leave on month-long breaks in the winter. It became clear as time went on that my father was excluded from the threesome. In fact, Elaina and Mom actually started putting him down and making little quips about him at family gatherings. He seemed to be getting older very fast as if he was wasting away. When I talked to Mom and Dad about it they said it was just aging. I tried to get him to a doctor, but Mom just cancelled the appointment. Everything seemed to be too much trouble for her. She and Elaina often got mad at Dad in front of me for not trying harder.

After one Christmas, Mom called and asked if I could check in on Dad while she and Elaina went on a week's vacation. I said I could, but I questioned the safety of Dad's being left alone. He was having trouble feeding himself and could barely get up and down the stairs. Luckily for all of us, Mom got sick and the vacation was cancelled.

Next came Easter dinner. I decided to ask the family out to dinner since our children were grown and off on their own. We met at a restaurant near my parents' house. I offered to pick them up, but they said they could drive that limited distance. Mom and Dad showed up without Elaina. She wasn't feeling well. I knew she was still mad about my questioning the vacation she and Mom had planned. After dinner, Mom and Dad ordered a take-out meal for Elaina. I just thought, "Typical, I'm supposed to keep my mouth shut. Pay for all the dinners. I certainly can't mention that Elaina is over-drugged once again, which is why she is absent."

Then came Mother's Day. My wife decided to make brunch and take it out to my mother, so no one would have to drive in my family. We arrived with brunch. We sat down with my parents and waited for Elaina to come downstairs. We waited over forty-five minutes with my mother making one excuse after the other for Elaina. Elaina finally came down and we sat at the table. My mother kept watching Elaina, saying things like, "Are you sure you don't want to lie down?" Elaina slurred her words more and more. Finally, she was bringing her hand to her mouth as if to feed herself, but had no food or fork in her hand. At this point, my wife said, "She is really overmedicated. We need to call an ambulance."

Mom said she had been doing this all week to punish her for allowing us to come to the house and bring her Mother's Day brunch. Mom and Dad leaned over her and said, "Elaina do you need to go to the hospital? You didn't like the hospital the last time you were there."

It was completely crazy. They were asking permission from Elaina, who was almost comatose, whether they should send her to the hospital. It seemed now that Elaina completely controlled my parents' home. My parents kept refusing to call the ambulance. We seemed to only be upsetting them. My wife and I left, saying that if she went unconscious they really should call an ambulance.

From then on I only dropped by to visit my parents with a call ten minutes before I was to arrive. That way Elaina couldn't punish them. I took my father out alone for Father's Day. I just didn't know what to do. My parents were getting older; my sister didn't work; things certainly weren't getting better.

I talked to my therapist. I knew Elaina was mentally ill, but she was arrogant and wouldn't admit it. She told me that she had too many assets to go on disability. I knew all her assets were really my parents. They had completely supported her for over seven years. They now were running out of money. They complained to me that they needed money, but I was concerned the money would just be used to enable Elaina. I knew they couldn't say no to her.

I'm worried about them, but I don't know what to do. If something happens to my parents, what will happen to Elaina? One thing is sure—I don't want to support her. Someone told me I could file an adult protection case against her for financially abusing my parents. But she and my mother are connected at the hip. That would devastate Mom.

This mental illness of hers is a bear. She can look good for brief periods. Yet she has caused me to loathe her for the pain she's caused our parents. I know they are also responsible for enabling her. I just don't know what the right thing is to do.

B. Helping Peter

Peter has a family that has more problems than just an adult child with BPD. There are many pieces in the family history that contribute to his sister's problem and the dysfunctionality of his family. His father was and still is an active alcoholic. His mother, who once was codependent and enabled his father, is now codependent and enables his sister.

The saddest part seems to be that the three of them have no use for Peter except when they have a financial problem or when they need his help talking to their doctors. According to him, they rarely ask about him, his children, or his wife. Instead, they call for financial advice. When he gives advice he usually has to explain it to all parties several times and, in his view, get his sister's approval. His mother and father seem to not be able to make any steps without the sister's agreement. He states, "She hasn't worked in twenty-five years, has no income, and yet her approval is necessary for them to even pay a medical bill." As he described it to me, it was as if in order to try to prevent her silent rages and sulking, the parents had become trapped in their own home. They were both enabling and being victims of Elaina's mental illness.

Peter is fed up. He dislikes his entire family but feels like he should help them. "Although they really have not been there for me or my family, I can't just ignore them. That would be wrong. However, now that Dad's health is failing, Mom and my sister want me to be their handyman, their lawn service, etc. I am always trying to figure out what I really should do and what they need to do on their own. If I let them, they would have me there three or four days a week, but I have work and my own family."

Peter complains that they have no concept of work; they often call him while he is at work and interrupt his meetings. For doctor appointments in which they need him to attend, they schedule the appointments around their hair appointments but not around his work schedule. They do not seem aware of what it is like to be Peter.

Peter therefore must protect himself by being clear about what he is willing or not willing to do. He is willing to help medically by interpreting the medical world, but is unwilling to be their handyman. He has tried to say he will not address financial issues with his sister, but she calls him anyway. Peter may just have to draw a line there and not address his parents' questions. When he does address their questions of what to do financially he cannot mention the cost of sustaining Elaina in her middle class lifestyle. If he does, he gets raging calls from his sister telling him "he's nosy" and has no business advising his parents. He is in a double bind because his parents are worried but do not want to change anything that will affect Elaina. At least if he says "I can't help you," he doesn't become involved with his sister's hysterics about his parents' income. However, his parents are running out of time and money.

Peter is left in a constant battle about the level of help to give his parents and what he feels will be too painful given their dysfunction. Peter and I have spent much time discussing what he has no power to change, and therefore should avoid or set limits, and where he needs to be of some assistance to his family. If giving assistance becomes too painful, given his sister, I have encouraged him to let it go and not be involved in those issues.

This is truly a family in which the serenity prayer from Alcoholics Anonymous is a part of each interaction. Peter constantly has to remind himself of what he can and cannot change and make his decisions based upon that assessment.

The first verse of The Serenity Prayer follows:

The Serenity Prayer

God grant me the serenity
to accept the things I cannot change;
courage to change the things I can;
and wisdom to know the difference.
                    —*Reinhold Niebuhr*

Peter has to evaluate his family from the perspective of understanding what things he does not have the power to change. He cannot change how they handle their money; he can only point out to them that they have choices. He can accompany them to medical appointments at times that work for his schedule. Peter is not his parents' handyman or lawn service. Peter cannot make them move to a home that is more physically appropriate for their age. Peter has quit trying to talk to them about Elaina's addiction to her prescription medications since it does not change anything. However, he did send a letter to his Department of Motor Vehicles with her name and car license number so they would remain on the watch for her driving. The letter helped him be able to let go of feeling responsible for her impaired driving and his fear she might hurt someone in a car accident.

Peter's life is riddled with moral dilemmas. He feels sorry for his parents. He would like to do more for them but is horrified by how they live. He is both worried about his sister and hates her. She seems to be sucking the very life from his parents, yet they seem to be volunteering to let her. He does not want to have to take care of her if something happens to his parents.

His mind has to practice self-discipline. Peter cannot think about where this is going. He has to take one day, one issue, at a time and ask himself: where does he stand today? There is no right or wrong, only what Peter needs to do to be at peace with himself and have a life with his own wife and children. He asks again and again, "How do I both honor my parents and myself?" Peter says he is not his brother's (in this case sister's) keeper. Only time will tell. If something happens to his parents, Elaina has no friends. The difficulty for Peter is deciding what level of compassion or kindness he needs to demonstrate so that he is at peace within himself. Peter did not create this mess nor can he unravel it.

Peter has had to grieve the loss of his idealized parents. It has become clear to him that his real parents are "empty," they have nothing to give him. They had little to give him as a child and less as an adult. In this case I am referring to the gift of nurturance and of validation. In chapter 4, I discussed parents as providing security, protection, importance, and respect. Peter has received only small doses of any of those from his parents.

Peter has not only grieved his own losses. He has grieved the loss of grandparents for his children. They have been there very little for his children. If there was a public performance like a play or a graduation, they used to attend if they were in town. However, even that changed after Elaina's last move into their home. It was important for Peter to realize his children did not miss their presence in their lives as much as he did. He had grandparents, good ones as he said; therefore, he knew what his children had lost, his children did not.

C. Sylvia's Story

I grew up as the middle of three children in a working-class family. Mom and Dad both worked. Because my older brother was busy with sports and after-school activities, I was always asked to go home straight after school to take care of my baby brother. He was six years younger than me. I was there, but I didn't know how to take care of him. Mom would frequently work the night shift, and Dad would be gone out with his friends. I'd have to yell at my brother to get him to go to bed. He would just yell back at me, and then he would complain to Mom the next day. Mom would then yell at me and tell me I needed to be a better sister. What did I know?

I ended up taking care of him three or four nights a week and often on Saturday. I was only twelve when I started. I remember giving up dates when I was in high school because I knew my brother wasn't old enough to stay home alone.

When I graduated from high school, I got a scholarship and left for college. My older brother was already married and lived in another town. I left knowing my little brother would be home alone a lot. My parents wouldn't change their routine. He was twelve and I figured he could handle it. After all, he wasn't my kid.

When I'd come home to visit I noticed my brother always had lots of friends. People were constantly around him and he got tons of phone calls. Actually, I was a little jealous; I was never that popular. I also heard from my parents that his grades weren't all that good. Mostly Cs and Ds. My parents didn't say much though. They seemed happy that he had lots of friends and that he didn't ask my parents for much.

When it came time for him to go to college, he enrolled in the local community college since his grades wouldn't allow too many other options. By then I had graduated from college and had been working a couple of years, so I sent him money to pay his first semester's tuition as a graduation gift. He continued to live at home with Mom and Dad and got a periodic job here or there but didn't ever work for anyone too long. It seemed now instead of being the youngest one to ignore, he was the one to worry about. My parents often called me complaining that he didn't do anything to help around the house and that he was always gone. It became unpleasant to visit my family because it seemed they were always yelling at each other.

In his third year at the local community college, his grades seemed to be a lot like they were in high school. He didn't talk about it, but Mom and Dad thought he was just wasting money. Then one day they called me and told me I had to come home. It turned out my brother had been arrested and was in jail. My parents didn't know what to do. They wanted me to solve the problem.

When I arrived at the police station, I found out he had been arrested with a mixture of drugs (cocaine and marijuana) in his car. The amount of drugs was so large he was being charged as a dealer. Of course, when I talked to him he denied being a dealer and said that someone else must have left the drugs in the car. I called my older brother and asked for his help. He simply replied, "Yeah I knew he'd sold some pot to the little brother of a friend of mine back when he was in high school. I guess he finally got caught." He had never told me that story. It finally all made sense. All those friends weren't friends—they were customers. The low grades, the whole pattern, pieced together.

He was sentenced to a year in jail. Dad asked me if my younger brother could move in with me when he got released. Dad felt sure I could straighten him out. He lived with me for about six months, got a job, then got his own apartment. For a while I thought things were looking up for him.

As time went on I noticed he had a habit of not working anywhere more than a year or two. He got married and hasn't worked for three years. His wife supports them, or so he says, but there seems to be a lot of spending and too little money coming in. I don't know how he makes his money. I can't care. It's up to him to figure out what the rules are. I've done as much as I can. This is now his life. I don't know what I'll do the next time he's arrested. I just want to wash my hands of all these problems.

D. Helping Sylvia

When Sylvia shows up in my office her issues are not about her brother with ASPD as much as learning to listen and take care of herself. She tells me the story of her brother as part of her story of growing up as an over-achiever victim, or in her case more specifically, a child who was asked to be a parent. She feels as if she has done her best but grieves the loss of the family she once dreamed she had.

Growing up, she believed her family was close. Now she realizes they ran on a no-talk rule and she knew very little about each of them. Sylvia makes the decision to try to honor her mother and father as they age and their health declines but to give up the responsibility for her brothers. They really don't talk to her much and she doesn't want to be the only one pushing the concept of family. These are difficult decisions.

She discusses her anger at her older brother for disconnecting and not being much help with their parents. Sylvia grieves these imagined losses less and less as she realizes it was really her work and dreams that created her concept of family, not what the brothers did. Sylvia has moved on to create a chosen family, one in which the members are mutually responsible and know how important connection is.

Notice that it is easier to help Sylvia than to help Peter. Peter has to deal with both his sibling who has the mental illness as well as his parents who both love and enable his sibling. At least Sylvia at this point chooses to focus only on her parents and herself. She has decided to separate herself from the sibling with the illness. Of course she is concerned about what the future holds for her younger brother, but knows she has no control over his choices. She has decided to focus on building a healthier chosen family with people who hold values common to hers.

Again, the situation becomes more complicated if the sibling has children or lives with the parents. I have seen aunts who are worried about their nieces and nephews whose parent (their sibling) has a personality disorder. If those children and the sibling with the disorder still live with the parents, that creates even more difficulty with boundaries and concerns for the children.

Relationships are complicated and there are no easy answers to how to handle a sibling with personality disorder. Again, you can only control yourself and make choices for yourself. You can choose to create a new family that nurtures you in ways your own family doesn't. You can decide to focus on your aging parents. No matter what you choose, you only control you. This is one of the hardest lessons in life to learn. Accepting that there are things you cannot change allows you to move forward to achieve a better life.

CHAPTER SIX

Having a Spouse with a
Personality Disorder

The following poem was written by one of my clients who fell in love with a woman with BPD. I believe it speaks for itself.

With one brief glance you stole my heart,
but through countless deceits you broke it.
No love can be built on falsehood,
and your truths were as hollow as the life you live.
Everything I had, everything I was, I gave freely
and laid it all before you.
But you trampled it underfoot without thought or care.
I enabled you to live your dream, while my life became a nightmare!
Now I see who you really are, I know the truth about you.
The façade has vanished like an early morning mist,
leaving only the cold, stark reality that everything about you was a lie!
You were NEVER who you said you were.
The only face in the mirror now is you and you alone.
There is no one left to blame.
Such an intimate betrayal cannot be met with kindness, or a smile.
So I abandon you to your fate, my dear,
though I pray for your healing,
knowing that at some point in my life I will forgive you.
I will never forget what you did to me and how it hurt.[2]

[2] Reprinted anonymously with permission.

In conversing with spouses who are now or have been married or are a partner to a person with a personality disorder, I usually sense a burden of shame. It's almost as if they feel bad for their choice, questioning if they should have known better. At the same time they almost always discuss the allure of their spouse or partner, especially in the beginning. They discuss a honeymoon phase where the person was on their best behavior. "It's as if she read my mind and dreams and seemed to embody most of the things I could have possibly have wanted." Then this same ex-husband says his ex-wife slowly began to display more and more craziness. "It's as if I was asked to adapt more and more. In fact, I adapted so well, always trying to fix the problems, always trying to be more and more understanding, until I realized there was nothing left of me in the relationship. I could have no needs. I then stayed on hoping to protect our children. Finally, I gave up even on that because her behavior was destroying them before my eyes."

The biggest difference in a marriage to a person with BPD or ASPD versus other types of relationships is that marriage is a chosen relationship. This leads to a different kind of guilt or blame. The person who married someone with BPD or ASPD is not only angry at their spouse or partner but are also angry with themselves for not knowing, for the choice they made, and for enabling the very behavior they despise.

As an adult you may marry or live with a person with BPD or ASPD. You may in turn have a child together. Besides the guilt and shame a normal parent feels, the non-SOS parent may feel even more guilt as he watches his child suffer from the effects of the SOS parent. This suffering includes emotional dysregulation from the chaos, from a role model of someone who says "rules don't apply to me," from the distortions, from the loyalty binds, and from being placed in the middle. The non-SOS parent will experience shame, fearing he has lost his child totally or at least portions of his child's life as a result of the splitting and loyalty binds placed upon the child.

A. Judd's Story: Married to Cindy with a Borderline Personality Disorder

I met Cindy while we were in college. I was a little shy and she was so outgoing. I was attracted to her right away. We lived together our last year of school. I was so in love with her. She was beautiful and smart. She seemed so sensitive and kind in the beginning. She seemed to complete me. Although Cindy was kind and seemed to understand me, I didn't at that time realize the price I would eventually have to pay.

After we graduated I took a good job with a large company in town. Cindy said she wanted to go to law school. I knew she was smart enough so I encouraged her to stay home, study for the LSAT, and apply to schools during our first year out of college. We were also planning our wedding so it sure seemed like she had her hands full. I would go to work and come home. The apartment was a mess, but I justified it given how much she needed to study. I'd come in and fix us dinner then sometimes she'd take a break to eat and sometimes not. She seemed grumpy a lot that year, but I racked it up to stress.

Finally, it came time for the wedding. We lived in the same town as my family, but hers lived in California and she didn't think they'd come to the wedding. She didn't talk much about her family. Once in a while her mother would call, but Cindy rarely talked about her dad. When she did talk, she would cry and say how abusive he'd been when she was little. She said he was so critical and unsupportive.

We invited them to the wedding anyway to balance off my side of the family. They all came—her mother, father, sister, and her husband. They gave us $5,000 to put towards the cost of the wedding. I was confused because they really seemed nice.

When they left, Cindy returned to saying bad things about them. She said they had really given her sister everything she ever wanted but had not been there for her. I asked her if she'd written a thank you note for their gift of money. She said she did, but now, with all I've learned, I doubt she ever did.

Anyway, she got into a law school only thirty minutes from where we lived. She was very busy during those years with her commute and the stress of law school. We really didn't get much time together. She would stay late for study groups. I went to work, then I would come home to take care of the apartment and do most of the cleaning. She was always so stressed. Cindy would be anxious about this test or that paper. She seemed to be in a bad mood a lot. Cindy also shopped a lot. Our apartment was stuffed with all kinds of knickknacks, clothing, and things. It was getting too small.

Cindy wanted us to buy a house, or should I say, she wanted me to buy our house. I tried to explain that between law school and her shopping we were at our financial limit. I told her if she'd cut back on her spending we might be able to save for a down payment. We argued a lot about money. It made no sense. She was so smart but didn't understand money issues; there were no limits. No matter how much she bought, she wasn't any happier. Cindy would just compare us to our friends who both worked and had already bought their home. She blamed me. She said I should get a better job or a second job. Personally, I thought I was doing well. We had only taken small loans for her law school as compared to most of her classmates.

I thought things would get better after she finished law school. After all, lawyers make the big bucks. She finished law school, but we still had to make it through the bar exam. She worked hard and passed, but we celebrated only briefly. She was upset. Friends of hers had gotten jobs with big firms, but all she had landed was a clerkship with a judge. She started work but was never happy there. She said the judge treated the other clerk better than her. In Cindy's world there were always problems and I was beginning to tire of them.

Cindy started going in late to work and leaving for lots of health appointments. She seemed to be ill often. I knew she was hired on a six-month trial so it didn't surprise me when she was put on probation at the end of the trial. Well, that just made Cindy madder. She went to the Human Resources people and told them her boss was abusive. From what she told me, this judge had had trouble with other clerks. She felt certain Human Resources would help. Instead, after speaking with the judge, they suggested she quit, so she did.

Cindy stayed home six months looking for other work. She was pretty depressed so I thought little of the fact that I was still doing all the work at home. She started seeing a therapist. During this time she made a couple of suicide threats. One day I came home to find her pretty mentally gone; I called an ambulance. They said she had attempted suicide and kept her at the hospital. The doctors changed her medication and she came home. I felt terrible for her. Nothing ever seemed to go her way.

She began to look a little better and started applying for jobs again. I became hopeful we could get back on track. She finally landed a temp job for attorneys. Instead of being happy, she was mad. Cindy thought the job was beneath her. Within a few weeks she began showing up late and leaving early. She always had reasons: she overslept; she had a doctor's appointment. Well, this job lasted only five months. I'm not sure if it ended or if she was fired.

At this point Cindy began to pressure me into having a baby. I thought it might make her happier so I agreed and Jen was born one year later. Jen was beautiful and I adored her. Cindy was actually kind of jealous of how I felt about Jen.

Cindy had been sick most of the pregnancy so I understood that she really couldn't work. We didn't even talk about her trying to get work. We moved to a larger apartment before Jen was born. Cindy was still spending. Spending now included tons of clothes, baby furniture, toys, etc., for Jen. It was clear we would outgrow this place soon. We were still arguing about money and Cindy was driving us further and further into debt. Finally, I cut up all our credit cards and Cindy was allotted only so much cash per week. I told her it was so I could begin saving for a house, but first I had to eliminate credit card debt. Cindy was furious. I found out later after we separated that she went had gone behind my back, gotten credit cards, and had the bills from those cards mailed to a post office box.

Jen was now one-and-a-half-years-old and cuter every day. Cindy stayed home with her during the day. I'd come home and the house was a mess, but she told me there was no way to clean with Jen around. After dinner Cindy would often disappear. She said she was meeting mothers from her support group at the Y or taking yoga classes. However, she was gone four or five nights a week. I would take care of Jen. I loved my time with Jen, but I began to doubt where Cindy went each night.

Finally, when Jen and I went by the Y one night, I discovered Cindy wasn't there. I followed her a different night and saw her go to a motel. That was it for me. I confronted her and told her she needed to leave.

I called my mother who often watched Jen during the day when Cindy had appointments. I explained what had happened. She surprised me when she told me she'd been babysitting Jen four and five times a week the last few months. Mom suggested she could keep Jen when I worked. I asked Cindy to leave and told her I would care for Jen.

Given her mental health history my attorney told me I should seek custody of Jen, and I agreed. During this time, Cindy would call raging at me and then a week later would call and beg me to take her back. I never knew what would be on the other end of the phone when I picked it up. I always tried to be nice but it was hard. Sometimes I was supposed to understand her problems, other times it seemed I was the source of all her problems. She'd go by Mom's to visit Jen maybe once a week, but Mom said sometimes she was in pretty bad shape.

Mom has since shared that Cindy told her I was rigid and controlling with money and that I was abusive to her. That was during the same time when she'd call me at midnight and beg me to take her back. Cindy also tried calling my brother and sister asking them for money and a place to live. Luckily they were all busy with their own families.

Cindy left to go back to California to her parents. She'd still call me to check up on Jen or to complain about her parents. Finally, I just stopped answering the phone when I saw it was her. I've taken Jen out to visit Cindy two times. She's in her own apartment and has held several different jobs.

After two years I've begun to date again. I'm scared to make another commitment. Jen is the most important girl in my life. I don't know what Jen and I would do without my mother. I'm terrified that Cindy could try to take Jen away some day. I don't know what to say to Jen about her mother. How do you explain a mental illness to a four-year-old?

Some days I'm embarrassed that I stayed loyal to Cindy so long. Some days I'm just thankful for Cindy, because without her, I wouldn't have Jen. I am worried what will happen to Jen if Cindy were to ask to have her for a visitation. I've heard the way she puts people down. What will she say to Jen about me or about my mother whom Jen adores?

B. Mary Ann's Story: Married to Luke with Antisocial Personality Disorder

After forty-seven years of marriage, two children, and five grandchildren, I give up. Luke and I have struggled most of our married life. The priest wasn't sure he wanted to marry us. We were young, but I was sure Luke was the one. He got a job after our marriage. It was a union job. Thank heaven. He might have been fired anywhere else. He worked there thirty-five years. But even I know his job was on the line several times. He was protected by his union membership. A few times they changed his hours or docked his pay, but he always had a job.

He has also always had his women. Luke would go out drinking in the evenings. He would go away for days on outings with the boys. He was always with a different group of friends. Sometimes when the couples would gather, one of the guys would start telling stories about this trip or that. They would be talking about what they did and things would slip. Luke wouldn't talk about it. He said I didn't hear them right. But that doesn't explain the time my doctor told me I had chlamydia.

I was only nineteen when I married Luke. He was twenty-two. He always treated me as if I was stupid. After our second child was born, I had a postpartum depression, which then seemed to give him the right to treat me like I was crazy. But I wasn't, I sought help. I remember talking to this one priest after twenty years of marriage and he said Luke wasn't the kind of husband Jesus wanted men to be.

I stayed home alone with our two babies without a car. Often, I didn't have money to buy groceries, and I had to beg rides to the pediatrician from neighbors and church members. Luke worked. He paid for the house and utilities, but that was it. As soon as I could, I started a little cleaning business. The kids went with me. That's where we got our money. I bought clothes for the children and myself, paid for their birthday and Christmas presents, and bought the groceries. Luke paid for the house and ruled over it.

It seemed Luke was always playing games with me. I'd ask him not to leave his pipe and tobacco on the kitchen table and he'd leave it there anyway. It was right where we ate. I'd move it and he'd move it back.

I'd ask him what he wanted for dinner. I'd fix it then he would refuse to eat it. I couldn't do anything right. After the children grew up, these games got worse. After he retired, he would sit up drinking (if he was home) until three a.m. and sleep until noon. The television would be blaring. I'd ask him to turn it down since I had to clean the next day. But he just turned it up. He'd also disappear for hours and come back, saying he'd gone for tobacco. But it was five minutes to the store so that never made any sense.

When the children were twelve and eight, I scheduled an intervention about his drinking. He went into treatment, but he never really quit. Things pretty much stayed this way our whole marriage.

I went to Dr. Linda after she'd helped a friend of mine. At this point the children were grown. My oldest, who was a girl, was in medical school. My youngest, a boy, seemed to be working this job and another but was living in a small apartment three hours from us. Luke would be nice when one of our children visited.

I had started sleeping on the floor next to our bed. I really couldn't bring myself to sleep in the same bed with Luke. Dr. Linda eventually got me to sleep on the couch. Then finally I started sleeping in one of the children's old bedrooms. She wanted to meet Luke, but I told her I was scared. I told her, "He knows how to look good to outsiders, which is part of what makes me feel so crazy."

Since my daughter had gone to med school, she suggested Luke be evaluated by a psychiatrist. The one part I remember was the psychiatrist saying that when Luke got angry he could get violent. Well, the psychiatrist didn't have to tell me that. Although Luke had never hit me, when he yelled at me, he would get right in my face and grab my shoulders or arms. I told Dr. Linda I was always frightened about that and the fact that Luke kept guns in the house. After I told her, she suggested the guns be kept somewhere else. I gave them to my brother to keep, and told Luke it was for our grandson's safety when he visited.

Luke went to volunteer for a senior program. He started bringing home televisions and other things. He'd put them in the garage, then they'd be gone. I asked him about it and he said it was none of my business. I was worried that he was stealing from some of the seniors he helped.

Finally, he was hanging out at the senior center with a forty-three-year-old woman who worked there too. He kept going over to her house to help her. She had three kids. One day her car broke down. Luke asked me for a loan to get her a new car. I told him, "No, she's not your daughter." He got mad and started screaming. He wasn't going to let me out of the house until I gave him the money. I finally wrote a check. I told him he had no business loaning her money and that he could either choose to work on our marriage or leave. He chose to leave. I knew he was having an affair with her. Since he left I've learned that he's over $60,000 in credit card debt. Where the money went I don't know, probably to support that woman and her kids.

I'm scared. I don't trust him. I've had the locks changed on the doors. The children are at a loss. After forty-seven years who expects their parents to divorce? I've got a restraining order on Luke. I'm afraid he must be desperate for money. I keep learning more and more, like the fact that he forged my name on a check.

I'm so angry at him I don't know what to do. I'm ashamed and embarrassed. I'm not ready to tell most of our friends. Luke must have been right: I really am stupid. Although on my better days I know it wasn't about being stupid; Dr. Linda reminds me I was brought up and still am a devout Catholic. I didn't believe in divorce. I was also always trying to hold my family together for my children. Even now I sometimes feel abandoned by my adult children. They hear me when I tell them what their dad did, but I see them trying to help him too. Dr. Linda says I can't make them choose between their mom and dad, but it hurts me that they help him. When they need something, they call me not him. I'm always working on remembering what Dr. Linda says, "A good deed for him is not a take-away from you." At least I've taught them to be good Christian souls; it just hurts sometimes. I am angry at him, and I want them to be angry too. Mostly I think they are just angry at me. I don't think they begin to understand how hard this has all been on me.

C. Helping Judd and Mary Ann

Both Judd and Mary Ann pride themselves on being responsible. They take pride in being loyal to their families. These are excellent traits, but both of them got to experience the dark side of those traits. Being loyal is important but not at the expense of being disloyal or disrespectful to yourself. Being responsible is great, but not when you have to be over-responsible for another adult partner. Being over-responsible allows and even encourages your partner to be under-responsible and vice versa. You become more capable, your partner less capable.

It is difficult because many do not realize they exist in a partnership without mutual respect and mutual responsibility. The shift to under-responsibility and disrespect is either gradual or was never there in the beginning. It is difficult to recognize patterns until far down the path. When they are recognized, the person may shut their eyes, feeling disloyal for seeing what he does not wish to see, for knowing what he does not wish to know—that his partner or spouse is not who he believed or hoped for or dreamed of.

To help Judd and Mary Ann, they need to learn to balance both self-respect and other-respect. They have the ability to place other's needs above their own. However, healthy relationships involve an expectation that the other also values and respects you; this is part of establishing belonging.

Many people think because they believe in mutual respect the partner will too. They have to know how to do it, not just talk about it. The other partner cannot learn mutual respect if it is not expected of them. Even then the partner may not choose a path of mutual respect and importance. They have to value the path of mutual respect too.

The issues of choice and responsibility make the positions of being a spouse or a parent different from being a sibling or child of a personality disordered individual. Some people feel they have made a commitment, a vow to remain in their marriage no matter what. They then believe they must adapt until they are asked to adapt to one too many dramas.

Many books might lead you to believe your only choice is to leave. An excellent book that gives ideas about how the non-SOS individual needs to change her own behavior is John L. Lund's *How to Hug A Porcupine: Dealing with Toxic and Difficult to Love Personalities*. Lund helps people understand the goal is not to change the SOS, but to become their best self, which may or may not include leaving. However, if you choose to stay you must learn how to set your own personal limits, how to disengage from dramas, how to avoid FOG attacks (defined by authors Randi Kreger and James Paul Shirley in their *Stop Walking On Eggshells Workbook* as attacks aimed to make you feel fear, obligation, or guilt). You must educate yourself to the dynamics of a personality disorder and the games people play for survival. It is vital that you have a support system, whether it is family, as Judd had, a therapist and/or a support group (e.g., belonging to the National Education Alliance for Borderline Personality Disorder or attending Al-Anon meetings for the spouses of alcoholics).

Bill Eddy, both a social worker and attorney, created the High Conflict Institute. He has written several books about helping high conflict individuals with their divorce. Often, although not always, when there is a high conflict divorce, one if not both partners have a personality disorder.

Eddy tries to teach both partners to use EAR skills in discussions. EAR stands for empathy, attention, and respect. Empathy involves acknowledging the other is upset and trying to connect to their feelings. Attention means *paying attention* to the content; attention does not mean *believing* the content. Respect means to remain respectful of the person even when you may disagree with the content.

Eddy has tools he provides couples that help them when discussing their children. These skills are meant to help keep children out of the middle of the divorce war. One technique is how to respond to hostile mail or email. It's called BIFF response: Brief, Informative, Friendly, and Firm. Another technique, "Yes, No, or I'll Think About It," is used to respond to a person without letting the other "push our buttons." These techniques and others can be found at www.HighConflictInstitute.com and are also useful in helping the adults prevent harm to their children whether they remain married or decide to divorce.

Remember, you do not control whether your partner uses these skills. The point is to use them so you can be proud of how you approached the issue. If your partner does not wish to change or to learn new ways of communicating, you can't change that. Many SOS's cannot change or change only much later in life after losing many, many partners. The change that comes is often made out of self-preservation, not from a desire to relate well to others.

One of the most difficult things in life is to understand you can only change yourself. When you work toward that goal you know you are not interfering with anyone else's wellbeing. You can also state with pride and integrity that you are doing all you can do. You let go of the need to change someone else and move towards being your highest and best self. You exemplify boundary setting and compassion, which is a role model for all who are around you, including your loved one with SOS.

CHAPTER SEVEN

An Adult Child with BPD or ASPD

What makes the relationship with an adult child with BPD or ASPD so different from the others discussed previously? It's because parents mistakenly believe they are solely responsible for who their children become. Some parents mistakenly believe that if they love enough, if they give enough, all children will grow into healthy adults. However, both assumptions reinforce the worst aspects of a personality disorder and are thus destructive to the long-term healthier functioning of their adult child.

At the very core of an adult child with personality disorder lies her need to control others. It seems easier to control others rather than to control oneself. The adult child will use any technique necessary to attain that goal. In attempting to control others, the focus is shifted away from the most important goal: learning self-control.

As stated earlier in this book, many professionals have been confused by their client's definition of physical or emotional abuse. At one time, professionals believed almost all people who had borderline personality disorder had been neglected or abused. More recently it is believed that one half have been abused. Formerly, in our work with clients with personality disorders, therapists missed the fact that some parents who were accused of abuse did not in any way appear abusive either in person or when hearing the family's history from another's perspective. Now we know, given the person with personality disorder's need to control and ability to distort, abuse accusations are rampant when this disorder is involved.

Kreger and Shirley discuss the tendency of people with borderline personality disorder to FOG; FOG represents the three weapons: fear, obligation, guilt. At the center of FOG is an implicit assumption: "I can use the techniques of fear, obligation, and guilt to try to get my way, but if you try to use them on me, I'll make you regret your selfishness."

The use of FOG is most present in the story of eighty-one-year-old Emma, who lived for many years off and on with her forty-eight-year-old borderline daughter. Emma first went to see a therapist a few weeks after her husband died. The only other time Emma had been to therapy was to accompany her daughter Zoe, who had been in therapy off and on for over twenty-five years.

By the time Emma went to a therapist herself, she was shrunken and depressed from her loss. Emma died only seven months after entering therapy.

Sue, her other daughter, knew I was writing about family members of loved ones with a personality disorder and brought me Emma's journals one day. She asked me if I could use them to help others. Therefore, I relate Emma's story with the help of actual quotes from her journals over the last nine years of her life.

A. Emma's Story: The Story of a Parent of an Adult Child with Borderline Personality Disorder

I am eighty-one-years-old and I just don't know what to do. My husband died five months ago. He really handled everything and I am lost without him. My daughter lives with me and has been back at home the last eight years. She doesn't work. She says she's sick. She's always sick. She's always going to one doctor's appointment or another. John and I often took her to the appointments. I don't understand why she doesn't get well.

Over the last ten years she's lived with us twice and at other times before that. It's been eight years since she moved back the last time. I don't know what to do. My oldest daughter Sue says Dad and I have enabled Zoe not to function. She's right, but she doesn't have to live with her—her moods, her sulking, her anger, her threats. I just don't see any way out!

NOTE: I will start the journal selections in 1999 to help you understand what it's like to be Emma. In 1999 Zoe, Emma's daughter, lived in Arizona with her husband but they were having problems.

1999:
First entry:

Lord, why am I so depressed, discouraged, and unhappy? Feel old and have lost my looks—why is it so important to me—help me to understand Zoe. She upsets me so. Why did I even have her? Shouldn't say that—will she come the end of May? Do I care?

Help me to keep my spirits up...Please

Later that year:
Lord,
I am sinking again—am in despair—worry constantly about Zoe—will it never stop.

Help me, Lord
Help, help, help

Note: By 2000 Zoe and her husband have separated and are divorcing so she is back at home with John, her dad, and Emma, her mother.

April 2000:

Angie had called about coming up north then Zoe called and is in a bad way so we're staying home.

Note: Here Zoe is controlling whether Mom and Dad can leave on vacation.

May 2000:

[Zoe, who had gone to Arizona for divorce proceedings, arrives back at John and Emma's home.]

Picked up Zoe at airport—came off in a wheelchair—she's in bad shape. She's in bed all day and won't eat.

Zoe was still in bed in a.m.—made her some hot cereal—guess I'm getting discouraged with her. She doesn't seem to want to get well.

Talked to Sue and told her about Zoe. Then told Zoe and now she's mad at me? What else is new? I give up with her—she is so on the defensive.

> **Note: This is an example of punishment for violating the no-talk rule.**

Later July 2000:

Went grocery shopping. Am losing it—all this confusion bothers me—Zoe is so short with John—doesn't like us being nosy—she should be on her own—am always tired—can't think straight.

> **Note: The example above is just one example of Zoe taking control of the household. Zoe's constant anger and irritability affects Emma's ability to think clearly.**

August 2000:

Zoe really in a bad mood! Didn't talk to us all day.

Zoe not feeling well—am so depressed—never ending—Lord are you there? Or am I being punished for something?

> **Note: Emma is very anxious that she is being punished for doing something wrong versus seeing that Zoe is acting inappropriately.**

> **Note: The year 2001 begins with Zoe living with John and Emma, then Zoe decides to move back to Arizona to look for a job.**

Late January 2001:

Am starting to worry about just coming home and facing Zoe—give me strength, Lord!

February, 2001:

Getting Zoe ready to move: we helped Zoe unpack all day. John is renting an extra place to store some of her things—she gets too overwhelmed and hard to live with!!

Did some packing of Zoe's things—lots of stuff!! She has so much junk.

Moved more stuff around for Zoe. Will it never end? Took more stuff in evening.

> **Note: Zoe moves to Arizona. Three months after the move, John and Emma visit Zoe in Arizona.**

Arrived at Zoe's about noon—surprised her getting there on our own—she still has a mess everywhere but says she's working on it.

How will we handle six more days with Zoe? She is so depressing. Why doesn't she get a job?

John and Zoe worked on boxes—took a load to recycling. We checked out mattress stores. We did buy one from Mattress Giant for $750. She had to have the best!!

> **Note: Notice that Mom and Dad, in their seventies, are doing the work of the move, not Zoe. They are also paying for it. They seem unable to set any limits and resent it. Zoe, like many with a borderline personality disorder lives in chaos and disorganization and is expecting her parents to take responsibility for her choices.**

During the visit:

She's worried about money. John's started moving boxes in Zoe's living room. Zoe and I went to get wallpaper. She picked out three different papers. John moved boxes in the living room and swept out balcony. We're both worn out from Zoe and her moods and wants—are giving her $3,000 to help out. Then we're leaving.

Another visit to Zoe's in October 2001:

Went to Zoe's at 9:30—John vacuumed and I dusted—can't seem to please her—now she wants rug cleaned—we gave her $6,000 but had the feeling it wasn't enough. She seems to be always in debt—

> **Note: This continues to document that the wrong people are being responsible for Zoe's life, both financially and physically.**

Same visit, John and Emma stay at a hotel when they visit:

Waited for Zoe to call—she didn't so we finally drove over and she didn't like it—cannot satisfy her—finally talked her into sorting a few things for Goodwill.

Went to say goodbye to Zoe—she's in <u>bad</u> shape. Feel guilty leaving her—am getting depressed too.

Zoe called again in a.m. all upset and crying—sounds desperate and what are we to do?

Am really down and no help in sight—Zoe spoke to Dr. and things don't sound good for the future. Fixed soup for all our lunches—Zoe is so resentful of everything.

A new decision—I'm staying here. John is going back!! Zoe seems relieved. Zoe is in bad shape—am getting exhausted.

Another bad day—Zoe is so groggy in a.m.—Zoe always wakes up so depressed.

John got me another ticket—I'm going home Sunday! Zoe is very difficult to be with—she picks on me all the time—will be glad to be home.

January 2002:

Zoe called and needs $700!!

February, 2002:

Called Zoe, a mistake—nothing but problems!! Needs money ($1,500)—I tried to nap but too upset. Will it never end—

> **Note: Does Zoe have a spending addiction? Where does the money go?**

March 2002—John and Emma are visiting Zoe again:

A long morning of waiting around for Zoe to get ready—we finally went to the store. Zoe made us wait until around 11:00 before we were all ready to go.

> **Note: Zoe has little awareness of how her behavior impacts John and Emma, and they function with a no-talk rule.**

Entry during visit:

John worked on Zoe's deck—put up some fencing—also took some stuff to Goodwill!

John finished his job on balcony—are both pooped and ready to go home—

> **Note: Again John and Emma have assumed the responsibility of making Zoe's home nice, not Zoe.**

After return from visit:

—are glad to be home—being with Zoe is stressful!!

Called Zoe and she finally called back in afternoon—she's really in a bad mood—I'm sick of it—I've about given up—help us, Lord

May 2002:

Zoe called and lost her job—was really down!! Which upsets me!!

June 2002:

Zoe called and said she had quit her new job already!! Guess I'll have to give up on her—she's determined to be depressed and feel sorry for herself—can't she see that she has caused a lot of her problems, Lord?

> **Note: Although Emma is aware of how Zoe contributes to her problems, she seems unaware of how she and John contribute.**

July 2002:

Talked to Zoe—she has a new "friend." Hope it lasts—hasn't a job yet—have faith!!!

Later in July 2002:

Zoe called in afternoon asking for money!!

One month later—August 2002:

I'm so discouraged—Zoe called and needs money so we wired her $500!! Will it never end—

> In October 2002, Zoe has moved back home to Mom and Dad. According to Emma they paid the movers to move her car and belongings home then they bought Zoe a ticket to fly home.

Middle of October 2002:

Another bad day—Zoe depressed—mad at us—we went to visit—Zoe really down—talks about not living—whatever we say is the wrong thing—help us, Lord—

Later in October 2002:

John and I went to shopping center, picked up a plant and candy for Sue, who is in the hospital—we bought food for Zoe's supper. Zoe, of course, was in a mood when we got home.

> Note: Zoe again is trying to control when or if John and Emma leave the house. She seems mad that her sister is briefly the center of attention.

Early November 2002:

Zoe is shaky again—wears me out worrying. What to do. I give up—she doesn't hear me when I talk—does she have brain damage or something? Zoe was weird this a.m.—not with it at all—she did eat oatmeal and then went back to bed...

Thanksgiving 2002:

Well what a day—Zoe became very shaky just before we were going to Don and Sue's for Thanksgiving. So we called her and said we'd be late. Zoe improved enough to go about 3:00 so we had warmed-over dinner—left for home early because John was nervous—what a day!

December 2002:
Zoe was dopey for awhile this a.m. Has to be her medication?

> **Note: Zoe is misusing and abusing her prescription medication.**

Early January 2003:
Am so discouraged, Lord!! Zoe doesn't get any better—is she worrying about getting a job and this is a good excuse for not doing it?

Early February 2003:
John's birthday!...Zoe sick again. We cancelled our vacation to Florida— lots of calls to make. Am resentful we can't go—should we put Zoe in hospital? What to do? Zoe is in bed all afternoon and we couldn't wake her for a long time—scary!! So hard on John and me.

> **Note: Zoe controls John and Emma by threats and misuse of meds.**

Separate entries from late February through end of summer 2003:
Zoe is gone again. We were going to brunch but decided not to. She finally admitted to overdosing. She gave me some of her meds to hide and dole out each day.

John and I want to go to Mankato for my birthday—Zoe says it's OK— Zoe really gloomy—am so sick of it!! Help me, Lord—she just lies around all day and it upsets me.

Zoe in a panic all day!! Help!! She's in bad shape. She was talking about going to the hospital but changed her mind—it's getting too much for me.

John told Zoe he'd give her $500 a month!!

Am so fed up with Zoe and her constant depression—can't stand it anymore—

Zoe decided she wanted to go to ER. Waited about six or seven hours— she got a panic attack and they transferred her to another hospital—for overnight. Am upset with her about it? What's wrong with her?? Still angry in a.m.—depressed—she'll never be able to cope on her own—we're stuck for life!!!

Zoe had an attack—just sort of blanked out—finally got her upstairs to bed.

Zoe really depressed (What else is new?) She literally wears me out with all her down thoughts!!

John and I went to Home Depot to look at garage doors. Stopped at McD's on way home. Zoe stayed home and sulked!

A long boring day—went to grocery store—suggested Zoe sort some boxes and she got mad at me—

Note: Zoe seems to hate it when Emma speaks the truth to her and expects anything out of her; therefore, she punishes her with anger.

Early September 2003:

Zoe got mad at us because we were having dinner with our friends, the Andersons—so juvenile!!

Late September 2003:

Zoe's birthday! She got cards from Sue, Di, Lynn, and Jen. Bought her some flowers—went out to dinner at Macaroni Grill. It was very nice and expensive. She was disappointed the restaurant didn't have what she wanted. I said something wrong and she was in a snit!!!

November 2003—John and Emma took Zoe to Florida for three weeks thinking it would help her. These are entries from the trip:

Took her along to Florida—

Have to do something about Zoe? But what!!

Zoe depressed!! But we bought her jeans, shirt, and purse.

Zoe depressed and angry. What else is new?? Help, Lord!
Bought a watch and may give it to Zoe.
A bad day—Zoe in a mood. Zoe impossible—help—help.

February 2004—separate entries by Emma:

Rained all morning, on and off all day. John and I went out for supper. Zoe didn't want to go, stayed home, had asparagus soup, which gave her diarrhea. Can't win—always something wrong with her—she's mad at me for saying Dad I are going to Florida—she is very depressed, but who cares?

What can I say about February!

Zoe was sick about 10 days.

> Note: Zoe uses various mild physical ailments, i.e., a sinus infection, cramps (these are the ailments Emma addresses in other entries) as a reason not to function.

The following are separate entries written by Emma over 2004:

Zoe woke up woozy—Zoe in bed most of day—get so upset with her—takes too many pills!! Have no patience.

Another bad morning for Zoe! Fixed her Malto Meal, which she almost couldn't handle—Zoe in bed all day—

Same as above—she is out of it most of the day—don't understand it... am getting depressed with Zoe and her problems.

What to do, Lord. Zoe has taken over our lives—all her problems are mine and I don't like it—

May has started out badly—everything revolves around Zoe and how her attitude is—not fair—am very frustrated!

Quit writing in journal because it was always about Zoe and her problems. So negative.

> Note: Although Emma seems to be aware of Zoe's problems, she is not aware that for her own good she needs to do something different too.

More entries from 2004:

A bad week—Zoe upset—her anniversary was the 15th—hateful and hard to live with.

Went to breakfast with Anderson's. Zoe in a bad mood—slow to eat and talk—had one of her blackouts in evening—we didn't sleep much worrying!!

Am having a bad week—Zoe is crabby and passing out, etc.—what to do??? Help, Lord—

> **Note: Zoe knows how to keep attention focused on her with John and Emma. Zoe clearly misuses her medications. There is clear agreement among professionals that multiple medications do not help people with BPD.**

2005:

> **Note: Emma quits writing in her journal. She states she is in despair in the note that follows and is dated 2005.**

Lord—

I am in despair! Nothing is right. I'm worried about my health—am so tired, depressed and see no way out of this life we're in. Zoe takes all my waking hours—wondering if she's OK—why doesn't she grow up?

Maybe it's my time to go?? What is your plan, God—help us!!

In 2007 when John dies, Emma makes this entry:

God—

Help me—I'm desperate—what about me and Zoe? It seems hopeless. Help me accept my life now. Amen and amen.

Only one month after John's death, Emma, at the suggestion of her oldest daughter Sue, went to see a therapist. Sue did not believe Emma would say anything about Zoe, having been punished by Zoe in the past for talking about her. However, Sue called the therapist and gave her some information before Emma came in. Sue was alarmed that her mother was shrinking, not eating, and not taking care of herself. Emma related to Sue that she talked in therapy about how she could take better care of herself. The therapist also referred her for an evaluation for an antidepressant.

I found the following note in Emma's journals. I asked Sue about it. She said it was written by Zoe on her last birthday while Emma was alive. Sue stated that Emma's therapist had encouraged Emma to take care of herself. So on Zoe's birthday, Emma was not feeling well and told Zoe that her therapist had encouraged her that it was okay to be "selfish" and stay home to take care of herself when she felt bad.

Mom,

Does being "selfish" mean you never do anything for anybody anymore? In all my years of therapy I've never been told to be selfish. Compassionate? Yes. But not selfish. Guess I buy my own Birthday Gift and go out to eat on my own if you're going to be selfish. You can look after yourself then. Your therapist is stupid!

Zoe used Emma's therapist's encouragement to take care of herself as a FOG attack (using fear, obligation, and guilt) to make her sick mother celebrate her birthday. Emma did not have the strength to defend against these strategies.

It is evident that Zoe had no concept that she had rarely been kind, compassionate, or understanding. She was projecting, blaming her mother for being selfish when she was really being selfish in relation to John and Emma. She had created a world with John and Emma where they rarely left the house without her for fear of facing punishment if they did. She was in her late forties, had no job, and did not contribute to the family household, either financially or through chores. When Sue asked Emma what Zoe did for her, she stated, "I don't know what I'd do without her. She locks the door at night for me." Emma had come to expect nothing and be grateful for anything. Emma died only two months after the above incident. Unfortunately, Emma and John had just left Sue to handle all of the Zoe problems.

B. David's Story: The Story of a Parent with an Adult Child with Antisocial Personality Disorder

I married young. I married a charming woman who, like me, liked to party. As time went on I realized, in retrospect, I spent too much time at work and we partied too hard on the weekends. My wife always seemed to need a lot and I drank a lot when not at work. My business was a success and we had James, a wonderful baby boy and the apple of my eye. When James was eleven, I realized I was drinking too much and checked myself into treatment. Afterwards, while trying to keep myself clean, I came to believe my marriage was a sham. I knew my wife had had one affair. It was the talk of the country club, and I wasn't sure about others. We went to marriage counseling but it didn't help. No matter what I did it wasn't enough, no matter how much I earned it wasn't enough. I wasn't getting any younger so I decided to leave.

James lived with her. He and I had some good times together but he seemed mad about the divorce. He was fiercely loyal to his mother. It wasn't easy. My ex-wife decided to move to St. Louis where she had family. I thought it might be easier on her so I said it was okay.

At first I didn't hear much except for requests for more money. James needed braces and played sports. There seemed to be lots of reasons to send money and I had plenty of money. After a couple of years I found a lovely woman and remarried. She was quiet and peaceful, very unlike my first wife. She'd been part of her family business and she had a good head for numbers. When James visited she always took a backseat, saying "I'm not your mother" and she "didn't want to interfere." However, she did notice that James wasn't always truthful and she talked to me about that. James would leave at night and not come back until three or four a.m.

She had a sailboat and I'd taught James to sail. She had asked me not to let James sail it without an adult present, but I didn't think there was any harm. One day James came home and said the sailboat had a problem. I went to the marina to check it out and the hull had a big crack in it. There were beer cans in all the nooks of the boat. But James said he'd found it that way. I had it fixed but my wife was furious.

The next problem came when I got a call from my ex-wife that James was turning sixteen and we needed to get him a brand-new convertible for his sixteenth birthday. When I told my current wife, she didn't think that was such a good idea, but it was my money and I did it anyway. James and my ex-wife had slowly become a real source of conflict in our marriage.

I remember when my dad died and I flew James up for the funeral. I rented him a car in my name at the airport to drive up to the funeral. He was only seventeen and my wife said I needed to send someone to get him. She didn't believe he should have a car rented for him. Well, I didn't listen. I was really tied up with all the arrangements of the funeral, and James came and went—where, I didn't know. But the rental company informed me that the car was returned with a big dent and I'd need to cover it.

James graduated later that spring from high school. His grades weren't all that good so he remained at home with his mom to start community college. I don't know how much he actually went since I wasn't there. For three years I paid tuition. I never heard anything about grades. He didn't work at a job and seemed to be gone a lot when I called him.

When he was twenty-one my ex-wife called me. James was being accused of statutory rape. His girlfriend was only fifteen. What he considered consensual sex, her parents did not. I hired lawyers and, with some cooperation from her family, we kept James out of jail, but he was on probation and had to go to treatment.

James went to work then for his uncle. He worked there for a couple of years and suddenly didn't have a job anymore. I was confused, and my wife pushed me to call my ex-brother-in-law. It was clear he didn't want to talk about it, but finally admitted there was a fair amount of money missing from the business. Although James said he'd been robbed, neither my ex-brother-in-law nor the police believed James. No charges were filed, but he could no longer work there.

At this point my ex-wife was telling me James's behavior was all my fault. If I'd only been a better dad… I sure felt guilty. James was charming and smart but wasn't going anywhere. She made it clear to me it was my job to straighten James out. My wife understood both James and me, and was scared I'd never been able to hold him to any kind of limits. She was terrified that James would drive our marriage apart.

That's when someone suggested we talk to Dr. Linda. When we met with her she talked about limits, what would be the rules if James came to live with us? She had questions like how would James contribute to our household and how long would he be able to live with us? I'd never thought this way. "He's my son," I said. Dr. Linda would reply, "He's an adult. What kind of adult do you want him to be?"

I felt guilty. I felt trapped between what my ex-wife told me I owed James and her, and how my wife and Linda were asking me to think. I was frustrated and angry. Don't all parents do whatever they can to help their children? James was my baby boy.

Linda didn't believe James was a baby. I said I would pay for him to go back to school. She instead suggested I'd already done that and it hadn't helped. Linda's suggestion was for James to pay and I would re-pay him for the cost of books and tuition if he got a C or better grade.

My wife and I finally agreed on a game plan, and I flew to St. Louis to explain it to James. James said I didn't have any right to give him rules. He said, "No." Since that time, James has been picked up by the police for driving without insurance and just now for dealing drugs. How could I have helped James? He seems to lead a double life—the one he tells me and the one where he looks for the easy way out. I've talked to Linda; she simply reminds me that James has to want to change his life, not me.

C. Bob's Story: The Story of a Parent with an Adult Child with ASPD

The following story is a composite story based upon at least three different stories that have been in the media in recent months. Although it is not a story in which I am clinically familiar, I thought it important to include in this section. With baby boomers aging, people living longer, and an increase in the prevalence of personality disorders, I believe these stories will become more frequent unless we educate the public.

Bob Morgan never bounced a check and always paid his bills on time. However, when this retired postal worker began to show signs of Alzheimer's disease and had a cardiac arrest, he gave his daughter Janet power of attorney and left it for her to pay his bills.

Over a thirty-three-month period, without her father's knowledge, she had taken $84,000 from his bank accounts. She was now facing trial for theft by swindle.

That alone would be too much for Bob to handle, but there was more. Because of Janet's actions, local authorities were trying to deny him of his government benefits, which helped pay for his care in a nursing home. A judge ruled that the transfer of funds was an attempt to hide funds so Bob could get government benefits. If that ruling stood, Bob would have no money and no place to live.

Senior advocacy groups were trying to help him legally. Clearly the money that Janet spent was supposed to go to his care. It was unclear how the money was spent. There was some evidence she used it to buy a new car for herself and to pay legal fees for her son who was accused of running a meth lab.

Bob said he trusted Janet with his care because she was the "smart one."

D. Helping Emma, David, and Bob

Emma needed the help of a therapist long before John's death. John and Emma kept taking Zoe to therapists, doctors, and psychiatrists hoping they could fix her. I would suspect John and Emma needed help when Zoe was a child. However, they did not seek help. Sue turned out fine so they didn't think they needed to change.

Sue became an over-achiever victim, needing little from John and Emma and trying to do life differently. She told me she saw how they spoiled Zoe, but it was more than that. Zoe was born with a sensitive temperament. John and Emma did not seem equipped to help her learn that her life and problems were her responsibility. As a child, they would comfort her through her moods instead of expecting that she treated others respectfully despite her mood and teaching her coping strategies to handle those emotions.

Emma seemed in her own journaling not to be able to understand and name feelings. Developing that skill early with children with sensitive temperaments is important. However, the second step is to help them understand they cannot abuse others with their emotions.

I tell children feelings can be like vomit. Feelings can be expressed in a way that dumps them on others and asks them to clean up for you. If you vomit on someone the least you can do is say I'm sorry. However, it's best to learn to express your feelings without making others responsible for them.

Zoe also needed help with her distortions. She needed help understanding that setting personal limits was not criticism of her, nor was it abusive. It was simply part of being in relationship; everyone has limits of what they will or will not tolerate.

These are skills that Emma needed decades before the situation had deteriorated to the writing in the journals. Zoe had become an expert at FOG (using fear, obligation, and guilt) and had split her family quite successfully. The saddest part of the story is that Zoe felt constantly unloved and abandoned, and yet she was pushing away those who loved her by hurting them emotionally. She did not have the capacity to see what she was given but instead dwelled upon all the things life, and her actions, had denied her.

Had Emma lived longer, her therapist might have had an option of educating her to the illness Zoe had. With each step of education, Emma would have taken a tiny step to set a limit. However, then Zoe would have worked even harder to bring Emma back to the enabling pattern that she now expected of her and to which she felt entitled.

When family members begin the process of personal limit setting, they must be strong enough to face the consequences. As seen in the note Zoe left Emma about her birthday, family systems work on the principle of homeostasis, which means to keep things the same. It is difficult to stop a pattern that probably existed all forty-eight years of Zoe's life. In that note, Zoe was fighting for what she thought was her survival: the need to get Emma to act in a way Zoe thought she was entitled to receive.

The steps to health are small steps and must always be made with knowledge that there will be consequences. Are you strong enough to help teach someone their life and their problems are their own? You, as a parent, can be beside the child on their adult journey, but you must not do the work of their life or pay for their life. Even if you are strong enough you will need support such as therapy and/or a support group. This is painful work. Do not attempt it alone. Al-anon has been really helpful for some parents.

In James's story you get another perspective. James's father David finally did set limits about the rules to live with him. Unfortunately, James's mother could not and would not. This was out of David's control.

In the end David is left with the never-ending guilt a parent feels when an adult child has problems: What could I have done differently? We cannot undo the past, but assuming responsibility for James's behavior in the present will further undermine James's notion that he does not have to change, others do.

Albert Einstein said, "We can't solve problems by using the same kind of thinking we used when we created them." James's logic is that "I should not be held accountable to any rules." He further believes it's okay to lie to David and then do what he wants anyway. While James continues to think this way, he will recreate the problems in which he constantly finds himself.

As a society we need to learn to discriminate between people who try to hide their resources and people who are victims of family members. Until we do this, the Bobs of our country risk homelessness in their most vulnerable time of life.

Teaching a parent to be brave enough to let a child fail and experience the consequences is hard. We all love our children and are fearful that the consequences may be too severe. Then we disable them by preventing or interfering with their learning process. This is not a loving act—it is a disabling act. I discuss this in my book, *The Journey of Parenting: Helping Your Child Become a Competent, Caring, Contributing Adult*.

You might be asking why I am dwelling on parenting. In many ways, the brain of a personality disordered individual never fully developed. Both with antisocial and borderline disorder, the people who have these afflictions do not comprehend or do not care about their impact upon the ones they "love." Therefore, many of my suggestions for the parent of an adult child with a personality disorder are no different than my suggestions for parenting an adolescent who may want all the privileges of adulthood but has not yet taken on the responsibilities.

LESSONS

CHAPTER EIGHT

Lessons from Therapy and from Within the Family

Whether we are therapists, family members, or acquaintances, we need to remember if we are speaking with a person with BPD or ASPD, we only have one small part of the story. We need to remember the SOS's tendency to distort and see life, through a lens of rejection in the case of BPD, or through a lens of control in the case of ASPD. Reality is probably not what they would have us believe. Their reality does not include their part or responsibility in the problem. Family members need to take into account their loved one's sensitivity and enormous ability to distort what is happening.

A. Lessons from Therapy

When Sue gave me Emma's journals she also brought me some therapy notes of Zoe's. Zoe helped little in cleaning the house after Emma's death. Sue brought me these writings of Zoe's and again wanted to understand what had happened in her family. She was furious that she was portrayed by Zoe as cruel and abusive. She wondered why Zoe's therapist had not questioned her more in her writings. Below are some journal entries you might find helpful in understanding the dilemma.

Late in 2003:
Zoe writes:

"I put up constantly with my father's blaming; sarcasm about who I am. When these criticisms get to me, I feel reactive; it's just a sign to me

that I am feeling very vulnerable. <u>My father and I have never had a good relationship.</u> I can let him go. It's just harder when I live with him. I have huge resentments towards him for how he wears my mother down."

> Note: If you've read Emma's journals you know John has given Zoe thousands of dollars to help her, built her a deck, unpacked moving boxes for her several times, and generally supported her. Zoe sees none of this. She is completely unaware of what John has done for her, but holds onto comments he might have made from fear about her future. Certainly all of John's comments were not benevolent, but Zoe does not recognize her responsibility in those comments. She blames him for wearing Emma down, but cannot see what *she* does.

Later Zoe writes:

"I've realized more and more that I've had a lot of power in my family. And my parents have always felt threatened. If I didn't have so much power, family members wouldn't spend so much time trying to "break me." It has been very painful."

> Note: When I was discussing the above entry with Sue, Sue couldn't understand. Her parents either wouldn't talk about Zoe or would defend her to Sue. Sue wondered if "breaking her" meant they had attempted to talk about the reality that Zoe needed to work since they wouldn't always be there to support her. Breaking her or being punitive to Zoe seemed to be any questioning of the distorted reality Zoe carried.

Zoe's action plan, which she stated in her therapy journals, was:

"Accept that I have a poor relationship with my family. Their criticisms come from their own feelings of inadequacies. Best to keep exposure to family to a minimum."

> **Note: Zoe lived with and was financially dependent upon John and Emma. There is no recognition of any responsibility she bore to them. In her distorted world no matter how much they did for her, they were critical and needed to be pushed away. This balance of the different realities needed to be addressed in her therapy.**

Zoe writes over and over again about being kind, but Emma's journals indicate that Zoe is rarely kind or compassionate to them or Sue.

Zoe writes:

"I am a compassionate, caring, and kind person. I love myself.

When I am aware of how difficult life is for all beings, how can I be anything but kind? Especially to myself.

My religion is very simple—my religion is kindness. Kindness and compassion begin with cultivating them toward myself."

> **Note: Sue pointed out to me that she also values kindness and compassion. According to Sue, Zoe was rarely kind or compassionate to anyone but herself. Sue states she was very self-absorbed and rarely saw the havoc she was wreaking upon the people who loved her. I have underlined the word myself above to demonstrate the self-absorption. Zoe does not indicate any awareness that she is neither kind nor compassionate within her family.**

Zoe writes:

"Sue stops by to see my parents and is often willing, even compelled to give me advice. She says things in a way that is alarming and frightening for me."

Zoe is advised by her therapist to say to Sue, "Sue, thank you for your advice. I feel I am working towards my physical and mental health. I would appreciate hearing affirming statements from you." Sue states she was simply trying to protect her parents from both financial and emotional abuse by Zoe. According to Sue, she had simply said to Zoe, "You need to get a job. Mom and Dad can't keep this up."

As John's health began to deteriorate, Zoe writes:

"Sue took my parents to see a geriatrician today. I didn't go but asked her to call me with the news. She gave me the news that Dad was in bad shape along with a threat that if my Dad dies Mom's income would go down and she wouldn't be able to afford to continue giving me money."

Later Zoe writes,

"I am stuck in the middle of wanting to let my parents stay in their home by giving them a lot of help, and a monstrous sister who doesn't want to be bothered and would be very happy to plop them in some institution."

> **Note: Sue was outraged since she was the one who was taking them to doctor's appointments and helping them in the home. Zoe was too overwhelmed to go to appointments; Sue had to leave her job to do it. Zoe would periodically help but the help was not reliable. It was clear in Emma's journals that Emma and John took care of Zoe, not the other way around. Instead Zoe blames Sue for not caring.**

This is an example of projecting. When Sue talks to Zoe about the reality of money, she sees it only as a threat, not as a request to help Emma.

After John's death, Zoe writes:

"Sue stopped by the house and I was home. She went over some paperwork with my mother, then she asked me to come down and talk. She began attacking me; her manner was abusive, shaming, demanding. I had not cleared my storage unit yet. Sue said Mom could no longer afford to pay for it. She said I was risking my mother's well-being. I told her I had enough of her attitude and went back upstairs."

Zoe's therapist advises Zoe to say to Sue, "Sue, I realize these are your perceptions. But I feel they are not mine. I am not comfortable discussing this anymore."

> **Note: Sue asked me, "What was I supposed to do? My mother could not say "No" to her. I saw her dying a little more each**

day. Why doesn't Zoe's therapist help her see her responsibilities? The therapist had to know she didn't work. Her money was coming from somewhere. Mom had always given her money but the money was no longer there after Dad died.

Zoe writes:

"I've been seeing a nutritional expert for the past two weeks. My mother makes comments over and over questioning: Do you have to be on this diet? Does everything have to be organic? It's too expensive."

> Note: Sue was further outraged when she read Zoe's entry about food. She told me she had watched her mother get thinner and thinner after John died. It was clear to Sue that Emma was both depressed and not eating. Emma, at this point, was still paying Zoe each month so Zoe could pay for her car and bills. Zoe did not contribute any money to the household for utilities, taxes, or food. Zoe is upset about what she sees as her mother's criticism. She refuses to hear Sue's concerns about Mom or listen to the real concern that her mother couldn't afford her diet.

Zoe again and again describes Sue as abusive when Sue was trying to discuss the real concerns both for her Mother and for Zoe. Zoe rates herself very strongly disagreeing with "My family really tries to help me."

> Note: No matter how much help Zoe received from Emma, Zoe negated it. Zoe's mind is completely made up that she has an abusive family who doesn't help her despite the concrete data around her. I am not saying her parents never got frustrated with Zoe. They obviously did, as Emma's journals and Sue's comments clearly indicate. However, they continued to support her in everyday life, often at their own expense.

Zoe, Emma, and John are all deceased now, but what can we learn from their tragedy? I hope it is clear all family members do not share the same reality. People with personality disorders cognitively distort their family life, their social interactions, and their physical pain levels. If we love someone who has a history of unemployment, re-employment, addictions (including eating addictions), inability to maintain social relationships, multiple marriages, then we must question if a personality disorder is in the room. If it is at all possible, the entire family needs help. Personality disorder is a family affliction.

Alan Fruzzetti (who wrote the book with Linehan mentioned earlier) is at the University of Nevada and has created a Family Connections program. It is a twelve-week class for family members to learn about BPD. One of the major features is to help family members learn the difference between validating and invalidating responses to their family member with BPD. A validating response includes:

1) Listening and paying attention
2) Acknowledging the other person's points
3) Working to understand by asking questions
4) Understanding the other's problem in its context
5) Normalizing the other's responses <u>when they are normative</u>
6) Treating the other as <u>competent, not fragile</u>
7) Matching with your own vulnerability (being true to how you too are vulnerable in the situation, not just the family member with BPD or ASPD)
8) Conveying understanding through actions

An invalidating response is:

1) When valid behaviors, especially wants and emotions, are regularly missed, misunderstood, criticized, or pathologized.
2) When invalid behaviors, especially passive or dangerous behaviors, are legitimized.

Sue told me she was careful when speaking with Zoe. However, Zoe, according to Sue, defined any limit she was asked to abide by as mean, cruel, and abusive. According to Sue, Zoe was never supposed to be told

"No." If she was told no, she complained that the person doing so was mean to her. Sue felt completely trapped by her sister.

Please note it is not invalidating to expect a person to assume responsibility for their own life if they are an adult. Instead, it is invalidating when family members are trained to expect incompetence and not speak about it. It is invalidating to treat the family member with the disorder as fragile, not competent. It would be validating for Sue or Emma or John to acknowledge that when the issue of fewer financial resources came up, Zoe felt abandoned. However, feeling abandoned and being abandoned are different. Zoe created her own abandonment when she refused to have any discussion about money as if the issue was simply one of perception versus concrete limits to how far resources can go.

Family members should not contribute to a no-talk rule within the family. Communication-skills training teaches that in important relationships if a person, due to whatever reason, feels they cannot continue a conversation, it is incumbent upon that person to designate a time they will return and continue the talk with the person initiating it.

The McLean Hospital in Belmont, Massachusetts runs a family group for multiple families. This program and others not mentioned here can help the family member with the disorder lead a healthier life. They can also help prevent triangulation and splitting of the family system by educating families to the dynamic.

B. Lessons Within the Family

We know from multiple resources that families with good boundaries, or limit-setting abilities, who are kind but firm, seem to have relatively good outcomes with family members who have a personality disorder. Families with no other addictions, like alcohol, spending, etc., have a better likelihood of handling the illness within the system. Families in which there are no other personality disorders do better, i.e., Emma was codependent to John first, then Zoe. The stories I have related are more like Shakespearian tragedies. In citing such dramatic tragedies it is my hope other families can recognize parts that feel familiar.

1. The Lesson on Denial

The single most important lesson to have learned in all the stories told in this book is that you cannot pretend this is not happening. It will not go away. To quote Zoe's journal, "I have a lot of power in my family." What Zoe did not understand was the power was not hers personally but was her illness. It sat like an elephant in the room. John and Emma constantly tried to pretend it wasn't there. Read Emma's journals. It was there, she knew it, but there was a no-talk rule. If we don't talk, we can all pretend on the outside it isn't happening. Zoe's illness became the vampire, which may have contributed to the weakening and eventual death of both her parents.

Naming is important. While Zoe defined herself as depressed and suffering from post-traumatic stress, she felt victimized, and yet she victimized all those around her. At the same time there was a double bind. "Don't talk about me or treat me as incompetent, but it is your responsibility, not mine, to give me all the trappings or rewards of a competent person. It is owed to me." That bind consumed John and Emma. If they would have named the illness and not enabled her to continue to live in the middle class world, would it have helped? No one knows. We simply know they died while trying to be over-responsible for the success of their adult child's life. The truth is no one can be responsible for their child's or anyone else's success or lack of success in life.

The question remains that if all family members had been involved in Zoe's therapy, the distortions held in check, the parents educated in both the illness and limit setting, would the outcome have changed? Again no one can say. Remember, SOS people think they are doing nothing wrong.

Harvard research and clinician Mary Zanarini says there are seven factors that can lead to earlier remission. The seven factors are:

- diagnosis at a younger age;
- a good vocational record;
- no history of childhood sexual abuse;
- no family history of substance abuse;
- absence of avoidant or dependent personality disorder in the family;

- high agreeableness;
- low neuroticism (not being overwhelmed by symptoms of depression, shame or anger).

Several factors were not in Zoe's favor. She had functioned vocationally only for brief periods of her adult life. She and Emma were codependent upon one another.

As for a loved one with ASPD, the same rules apply. If you are in a relationship in which you can do nothing right, in which you are never enough, ask yourself what part is really yours and what part is your partner's. Does he have to have control of everything? I've seen people with ASPD control the thermometer in the home, the amount the partner can drive, and more. Be careful when one person in the relationship constantly makes you feel at fault, makes you feel you are not enough.

To move out of denial, family members must both recognize and accept the illness for what it is. They must be compassionate, but with limits for how much responsibility they will take for an adult child, for a spouse, for a sibling, or for a parent, or how much control they will give away to those loved ones.

2. The Lesson of Boundaries or Limits

In their workbook, Kreger and Shirley are very clear that the word "boundary" seems to bother some people. "Personal limit" sounds less threatening to loved ones with BPD and non-BPD. It is their experience that the word boundary may trigger feelings of abandonment in the person with BPD. Certainly, in the loved ones with ASPD, boundaries trigger anger about the loss of control.

Let me cite another example between Zoe and Sue. After Emma's death, Sue came in to see me. Zoe was pressuring Sue to let her live with Sue's family. According to Sue, Zoe tried to guilt her, reminding her that Sue's family had often hosted foreign exchange high school students in the past. Sue was scared because she did not trust that Zoe would ever leave without a struggle once allowed to live with them. Sue did not want Zoe to live with her family, but she was scared to say "No"; scared that Zoe couldn't live on her own.

At the time Sue's daughter was having some medical issues and Sue did not feel she could handle one more stressor. I coached Sue to say to Zoe, "Yes, I have invited others to live with us in the past, but that simply doesn't work for us now." Zoe was obviously angry, but Zoe was clearly not Sue's responsibility. After Emma's death, Zoe did move out to an apartment and lived there.

Sue struggled with the Judeo-Christian teaching that you are your brother's keeper. To what extent? How much responsibility does Sue hold for Zoe's life? If she were to allow Sue to live with her family, she would need very clear limits, such as how long Zoe could stay, what Zoe's responsibilities would be in Sue's household, and what would occur if those responsibilities were not met. Given the history between Sue and Zoe this discussion alone might be considered cruel and abusive. Remember, Zoe had led most of her life without expectations.

There are several religious teachings that family members need to resolve within themselves. My friends who have better training in theology tell me the brother's keeper teaching is more about our treatment of humanity. It is not meant to be literally translated as your family brother or sister.

Another religious teaching is: "Love is patient. Love is kind." Sometimes the word "patience" is interpreted to mean "no limits." I would assert that patience is part of the problem in many families I have seen. In setting no limits, the family member eventually became mad or rageful and said or did things they regretted later. In my book, *The Journey of Parenting*, I quote Ada Alden, a parent educator, who says in parenting "too much water kills the plant." In other words, love without limits can kill the growth of a healthy adult. In the case of dealing with a loved one with BPD or ASPD, it is important to realize that too much patience can enable the illness to become more and more distorted. Then, when you lose your patience, you act in an unkind way, or in a way you feel is unkind. You feel guilty. Due to guilt you become too patient again, and the cycle begins anew.

Unconditional love does not mean love with no expectations from another adult. Love involves mutual respect with both parties honoring the other's limits. It is not unidirectional as it was with Zoe where everyone catered to her but were not even allowed to speak of her responsibilities in return.

A third teaching based upon our religious traditions is "Honor thy father and mother." We all share a responsibility to our parents, even if they have this illness. What are the limits of this responsibility? It is not a child's responsibility to make a parent happy. In fact, not even an adult can make any other person happy all the time. As an adult, we must ask ourselves, how much can I do or give freely to my parent with no expectations in return? This may be different for different siblings within the family. Do not compare your giving to your sibling's giving. If you have children, you must also ask yourself: What do I wish to teach my children with regard to honoring their elders? These questions are difficult to answer but will guide you to your own personal limits.

Another Christian religious tradition is to "turn the other cheek". An interesting interpretation of this tradition is a family member who believes forgiving and forgetting are the same thing. It is always important to forgive our transgressor. Forgiving is letting go of expectations that things would be different than how they were or are, not forgetting how they were or are. Not forgiving only leaves anger within you, which hurts your health, not the person who has wronged you. However, to forget, to pretend it didn't happen, and for you to do the same thing again and again and expect a different outcome is craziness.

John and Emma repeatedly gave Zoe money and bailed her out of her debts. Emma clearly resented doing so, but she and John did not say, "No." How would it have changed if they set up a repayment plan, which, if not met, would mean they would not give future loans?

Albert Einstein is often quoted as saying, "Insanity is doing the same thing over and over again and expecting a different outcome." Remember to ask yourself if the person with whom you are dealing has learned from their mistake. You cannot change them. Your only power is in changing yourself. People with personality disorders blame others for their problems. They accept little or no responsibility for making the internal changes needed to not recreate the problem. A person with antisocial personality disorder steals from the business and blames it on "the boss who makes too much money and I need to get mine too" or "society who is unfair to the average Joe." As long as a person with ASPD holds this distorted logic, they will recreate their same problems.

In their workbook for loved ones of people with BPD, Kreger and Shirley discuss myths that get in the way of the person's functioning with personality disorder. Their list is extensive and I will not discuss it all here. The one myth I have seen trap family members most often is that "love conquers everything." In John and Emma's case they clearly believed if they loved enough, did enough of what Zoe wanted, she would get well. They hoped that Zoe having enough would lead her to step forward and take responsibility for her life. They hated conflict and tried to avoid it at all costs, including stopping their vacations and outings. As Kreger and Shirley say, "If you take responsibility for the BPD's chaos, you risk reinforcing that behavior and causing yourself a lot of grief. If you let the BPD handle her own problems, it's more likely she'll learn how to take care of things herself or avoid dramas altogether."[3] John and Emma confused loving another with taking responsibility for another adult.

With a loved one with ASPD the same rules apply. I teach parents that if a child is yelling or aggressive they must disengage from the child. If they remain engaged, they inadvertently teach the child to mistreat those who love them the most. The same rules apply to adults. It is a misinterpretation of "love bears all." Adults need to be responsible for how they treat those who love them.

3. The Lesson on Enough

For whatever reason, the brain of someone with a personality disorder does not recognize when it has enough. This could be enough love, money, drugs, attention, sex, food, control, alcohol… The list goes on and on. They seem to work from a nullification principle. In other words, they nullify whatever they do have or are given. They do not remember or recognize it except for brief moments.

---

[3] Randi Kreger and James P. Shirley, *The Stop Walking On Eggshells Workbook*, Oakland, CA: New Harbinger, 2002, p. 97.

What seems to capture most of their attention is the negative: what they do not have or are not given. Peter in his story had to make decisions about how much work or time he could give his parents and sister. Emma could not give Zoe enough money or attention. No matter how much Zoe received she defined her family as being unsupportive.

The converse of the nullification principle is also true. The loved one with BPD or ASPD notices what is done to them or around them that feeds the story within them of abuse or abandonment. This is a sad way to live: to not notice what they might have been given but instead to constantly focus upon the themes that reiterate their fears of abandonment or loss of control.

The lesson of enough, when you have a loved one with BPD or ASPD, has to be within you. What can you give with a free spirit and a good heart? Does your giving interfere with the growth of your loved one into a healthier, more contented adult?

You cannot base what is enough on what the family member says or does. The limit must come from within yourself. You need to communicate that you have not abandoned them nor are you responsible for their happiness. You need to communicate that they cannot control you but instead need to work on controlling the fears within their own selves.

4. The Lessons About Guilt: DO NOT FEEL SORRY FOR YOUR CHILD, SIBLING, SPOUSE, PARENT

Feeling sorry for your family member interferes with your ability to set good personal limits. I am not saying you cannot say, "I am sorry this or that happened." But you must remember that the incident being described is *their* perception; recognize that they may be distorting reality. You must address their feelings, alternative perceptions (*could it be...?*) and, if they wish, offer assistance in problem solving. After that, you need to disengage. Vampires feed on caretakers. They feed on people who <u>need</u> to be kind, who <u>need</u> to solve others' problems. These are adults who <u>need</u> to learn to solve their own problems. They feed on people feeling sorry for them.

Feeling sorry for a person makes you, as a loved one, do too much to help. Most psychologically healthy people do not want others' pity. Most disabled vets, for example, do not want pity. They want assistance only so they can function on their own. In contrast, some people with a personality disorder have permanently claimed the victim role within the family. No one can be sicker. No one deserves attention more than they do—giving attention to anyone else is seen as a take-away from them.

When discussing her work on victim typology, psychologist Noel Larson once said, "There are some victims to whom I will not hand a Kleenex. It is important that she reach for it herself." Noel is a kind, compassionate therapist. She has identified that victims with a personality disorder need clear limits on how kindness is expressed, for they constantly seem to need to be a victim. In her office, she wanted to be empathetic but did not want to reinforce victimization.

A loved one with ASPD will not acknowledge or accept their need to control or their responsibility in the problem. If you are feeling sorry or guilty, think of how they may have placed you in the trance of their story. David Mays, MD, who works with people with ASPD, states no one should work with them without a team. An ASPD person is so good at conning professionals into believing that they need to be an exception to a rule, anyone dealing with such people must always have others to help break the trance.

Finally, given that these people are part of the family, remember that a family cannot be made for an adult. Adults have to want a family and be willing to take up the responsibility and reciprocity inherent in belonging to a family. These illnesses allow little room for that as the person with BPD or ASPD does not have the ability to think about other family members' needs. The question is, does the SOS want to develop that ability and is the SOS willing to sustain the work to develop that ability?

5. The Lessons on Conflict Avoidance and Secret Keeping

You cannot avoid conflict because the loved one with BPD or ASPD becomes mad when you exercise a personal limit or expect respect in return. If you speak about them, especially when they are not present, they do not have control of what you say. Therefore, they are mad. However, in order to try to get your bearings in a crazy, chaotic world, you must speak. You may talk to a friend, to your own spouse, to a therapist, to a minister, or anyone else who you think can help you. You cannot allow the loved one with BPD to believe they get to control what you talk about with others.

This conversation must remain respectful. The talk must not be with the intention of putting your loved one down. The intention needs to be for your support and assistance in understanding how to best set limits. The support is needed so you can respond using your highest and best self.

Secret keeping is one sign of a very unhealthy relationship. I tell children in my office that the only secrets we keep are happy secrets, like what we're getting someone for Christmas. Secret keeping is one variation of the no-talk rule, but it is used as a way to split or triangulate families. This is not okay for children, grown-ups, or anyone in a loving family.

As for the conflict that erupts when you choose not to be controlled, remember your loved one needs to learn that the only person they can really control is themselves. This is hard to do, but you must ignore their tantrums. You must be okay with asking for what you need in return. You must be okay with giving a response like, "This won't work for me." You must learn to reframe their interpretations of what your behavior means to them. You must be okay with telling them what you intended versus how they heard you. At the same time that you validate their right to feel a certain way, you need to validate your right to disengage from their anger and your need for the mutual respect.

If you are familiar with parenting an adolescent, the above strategies in handling conflict are familiar. They are the same ones I and many other parenting specialists suggest during those adolescent years. What you cannot do is think if you do what they want, the conflict will end. There is never enough, because at their core they are terrified they are not really enough: human or lovable. Remember, vampires have an illness. Edward, the vampire in *Twilight*, is loved because he holds himself to limits. Edward, unlike the human-blood-drinking vampires, does not destroy the person he loves—he protects her. People who have a personality disorder must hold themselves to basic limits to be able to live within human society.

6. The Lessons of School and Being a Student

A person with a borderline personality disorder or an antisocial personality disorder can be very smart. After all, they are usually good at finding a way around the work of life or the rules of life to get what they believe they deserve. This intelligence can often be seen when they are in school. They can be very good students. Being a good student does not require the same kind of sustained work an 8 to 5 job requires. College students are not in classes all day. There are periods of sustained work and periods of breaks. The professor is usually pretty clear about assignments and expectations. Students are coached on how to complete the work. Classes and professors change each semester, leaving little time for the development of social problems while in those settings.

In contrast, the work setting involves continuous stress each day. The world of work often requires independence regarding managing the details of doing work. This can lead to anxiety, blaming, and much drama by a person with a personality disorder. Working day after day with the same people allows for the development of conflict and drama within the workplace, just like conflict develops with the family.

Because people with BPD and ASPD on some level recognize the above-mentioned factors, some adults with personality disorders would just like to stay in school. Especially if they have tried to make it in the real-work world. There needs to be financial limits on how long the family or our society supports training when training is not used for later real-work-life functioning. Again, for therapists and family members, the history of the person involved speaks volumes.

7. The Lessons About Change

The most difficult and most important lesson to learn when dealing with an SOS is to let go of all expectations to change the SOS. Expectations, as John Lund says in *How to Hug A Porcupine*, are simply wishes. You can wish all day long, but expectations make you angry when they are not met. You *cannot* control another person's behavior. You *can* control your own.

What do you value? How do you interact with this person in a way that honors what you value and who you want to be? Do you want to be a bully or manipulator? No. Then you must think about how to respond or go about your goals using integrity and respect. What I am saying is difficult; when someone is throwing mud it is all too easy just to become a mud thrower. However, that will leave you feeling as bad about yourself as you feel about the SOS.

Instead, you need to consider how you can speak, act, and write in such a way that feels as if you honor your best self. You may have to discuss your points with a third party. You may have to have someone edit your emails before you send them. Bill Eddy of the High Conflict Institute standardly has all his brief, informative, friendly (BIFF) emails edited. Each time they are edited, he says they improve.

This process is not meant to change the response of the SOS. It is meant to leave you with a sense that you did all you could do. It is meant to leave you knowing you have approached an important issue in a respectful way.

I am not in any way saying you can change your loved one. Once you think that, you are stuck in a circle of doubt about what you need to do to make her respond differently. That is codependence.

Her response is hers. You can only be responsible for your response or choices about what you want for your future.

C. In Summary: The Lesson of Hope

I have written many different stories in this book. Some are written from my perspective. Others are written from the point of view of the family member. Some are poems written and donated by real family members. Finally, there are the excerpts from a mother's journals, and the journal of her borderline daughter.

The brain is remarkable. People do the same thing again and again. Only when the brain recognizes a behavior that is destructive to itself or its loved ones is there an opening to change behavior. Some people do not seem to recognize when their same behavior creates the same problem again and again. However, they do seem to recognize when someone else's behavior might create or sustain problems.

Reading so many different stories you might recognize something you have done as a family member that was not helpful for you or for your family member. You may even be able to pat yourself on the back for handling a situation sooner or better than in a story. My hope in writing this is that family members will recognize the unhelpful patterns in the stories that are familiar, and then possibly even make a different choice in their lives.

The stories in this book are sad. It has been hard to write them feeling the pain of each family as I wrote. However, it is not my intention to leave you, the reader, hopeless. Hope is the salve of love. As stated previously, love alone cannot change your family member. Love with compassionate limits is the answer. This answer is to help you change your behavior so you can retain your self-respect while interacting with your loved ones.. The answer lies in knowing your limits in order to allow the SOS to change himself.

Hope allows you to continue on your journey with your family member. In my experience, hope is most resilient among the children and parents of a family member with a personality disorder. All children carry an eternal hope that one day the parent with a personality disorder may be there for them, as opposed to the adult child still needing to be present for the parent. The adult child sets limits on her expectations and how often or for how long she will visit the parent. However, a small glimmer of hope within still looks for some positive comment from her parent. When those brief moments come, she will need to remind herself that moment may be all her parent can do. Her parent will never be the parent she has dreamed of and yearned for.

As for the parents of the adult child with BPD or ASPD, they, too, hope. They want happiness and success for their child. The parent must learn not to sabotage the growth of the adult child by giving or doing too much. Real hope comes from recognition of the history and belief that in each case the SOS has the opportunity to be competent. False hope is the same as denial. With the denial comes forgetting.

Forgetting is not the same as forgiveness. Forgetting leads to the same problems repeating again and again. Not being in denial leads to a place of acceptance. Acceptance gives a constructive path for you out of the destructiveness of an SOS. Acceptance on your part helps quell the anger. It does not change your adult child; only he can do that.

With acceptance, the parent will recognize the hope and hold fast to constructive limits that may feel unkind. The parent may even hear from the adult child that the limit is unkind or even abusive. Hold fast to the hope that with limits the adult child can grow into a competent adult.

Always treat the adult child as a competent person, giving the SOS the option to fulfill your dream.

Hope seems to die quicker among the partners, spouses, or siblings because they are tired and they seem to have more choice. Therefore, in this group it is my experience that although they may love the person with BPD or ASPD, they lose hope that anything can change. Partners, spouses, and siblings who lose hope either disconnect or decide to keep distant from their loved one in order to survive. Relationships require mutual reciprocity. The SOS individual does not recognize other; hence, partners, spouses, and siblings often just give up or limit the interaction.

In *The Journey of Parenting*, I explain the channels, the shoals, and how to know if you are headed out of the channel. My concern in writing both this book and *The Journey of Parenting* is that our society seems to value dysregulation and not to value limits or reciprocal respect either for our children or ourselves. For this and other reasons I believe more people are developing personality disorders, or at least the traits. Children are allowed to grow up out of the channel. Special, sensitive children are being born with temperaments that lead them to distort the world in which they live and the people who love them. This is heritable. What we do with those traits is up to us.

We, as parents, cannot control it all. We cannot control some of the traumas our children experience, but we can help with the definition of that trauma. In so doing we steer them back closer to the channel.

In *Twilight*, Edward is a vampire. His family, however, has decided to live among the humans and not feed on human blood, to feed only on animal blood. It is difficult, but they do it.

It is difficult to work with the distortions of a loved one with personality disorder. To successfully live amongst us, they must be able to feel the love they are offered and to not push it away. It is my greatest dream that families learn and are assisted in guiding the family to a healthy, satisfying life. In order to do this they must differentiate between a wish they hold for the loved one's behavior versus the expectation for the loved one to change. It is my hope that doing so will prevent some of the pain that I have witnessed and related to you in this book. That alone would make this work worthwhile.

Diagnostic criteria for 301.7 Antisocial Personality Disorder (ASPD)

A. There is a pervasive pattern of disregard for and violation of the rights of others occurring since age 15 years, as indicated by three (or more) of the following:
   1) failure to conform to social norms with respect to lawful behaviors as indicated by repeatedly performing acts that are grounds for arrest
   2) deceitfulness, as indicated by repeated lying, use of aliases, or conning others for personal profit or pleasure
   3) impulsivity or failure to plan ahead
   4) irritability and aggressiveness, as indicated by repeated physical fights or assaults
   5) reckless disregard for safety of self or others
   6) consistent irresponsibility, as indicated by repeated failure to sustain consistent work behavior or honor financial obligations
   7) lack of remorse, as indicated by being indifferent to or rationalizing having hurt, mistreated, or stolen from another
B. The individual is at least age 18 years.
C. There is evidence of Conduct Disorder (see p. 90) with onset before age 15 years.
D. The occurrence of antisocial behavior is not exclusively during the course of Schizophrenia or a Manic Episode.

DSM IVR

• Diagnostic criteria for 301.83 Borderline Personality Disorder (BPD)

A pervasive pattern of instability of interpersonal relationships, self-image, and affects, and marked impulsivity beginning by early adulthood and present in a variety of contexts, as indicated by five (or more) of the following:

1) frantic efforts to avoid real or imagined abandonment. **Note:** Do not include suicidal or self-mutilating behavior covered in Criterion 5.

2) a pattern of unstable and intense interpersonal relationships characterized by alternating between extremes of idealization and devaluation

3) identity disturbance: markedly and persistently unstable self-image or sense of self

4) impulsivity in at least two areas that are potentially self-damaging (e.g., spending, sex, substance abuse, reckless driving, binge eating). **Note:** Do not include suicidal or self-mutilating behavior covered in Criterion 5.

5) recurrent suicidal behavior, gestures, or threats, or self-mutilating behavior

6) affective instability due to a marked reactivity of mood (e.g., intense episodic dysphoria, irritability, or anxiety usually lasting a few hours and only rarely more than a few days)

7) chronic feelings of emptiness

8) inappropriate, intense anger or difficulty controlling anger (e.g., frequent displays of temper, constant anger, recurrent physical fights)

9) transient, stress-related paranoid ideation or severe dissociative symptoms

DSM IVR

155

Changes to Come In DSM5

In May, 2013 the American Psychiatric Association will publish the updated version of our Diagnosis and Statistical Manual, DSM-5. Changes are currently under discussion and may change again as I write this as there are several lawsuits that could affect its final version.

Currently DSM-5 eliminates the Axis I, II, III, IV, and V descriptors, which may help in some of the problems I have described. In the proposal therapists have up to six months to diagnose and then shall rate the disorder according to its severity, 0 (no impairment) to 3 (severe impairment).

Six personality disorder types are defined: antisocial, avoidant, borderline, narcissistic, obsessive-compulsive, and schizotypal. There is also Personality Disorder Trait Specified (PDTS) which replaces Personality Disorder Not Otherwise Specified. The committee at this point is changing the way personality disorder is defined. Personality disorders will be specific to impairments in personality (self and interpersonal) functioning and the presence of pathological personality traits. The traits designated under ASPD are antagonism (characterized by manipulativeness, deceitfulness, callousness, and hostility) and disinhibition (characterized by irresponsibility, impulsivity, and risk taking). The traits designated under BPD are negative affectivity (characterized by emotional liability, anxiousness, separation insecurity, and depressivity), disinhibition (characterized by impulsivity, risk taking) and antagonism (characterized by hostility).

Again, this model is still under discussion and is therefore subject to further revision..

Resources

Aguirre, Blaise <u>Borderline Personality Disorder in Adolescents: A Complete Guide to Understanding and Coping When Your Adolescent has BPD</u>. Beverly, MA: Four Winds Press, 2007.

American Psychiatric Association, <u>Diagnostic and Statistical Manual of Mental Disorders, Fourth Edition</u>. Washington, DC, 1994.

Bateman, Anthony and Peter Fonagy <u>Mentalizaion-based Treatment for Borderline Personality Disorder: A Practical Guide</u>. NY: Oxford, 2006.

Beattie, Melody <u>Codependent No More: How to Stop Controlling Others and Start Caring for Yourself</u>, New York: Harper and Row, 1996.

Bernstein, Albert <u>Emotional Vampires: Dealing with People Who Drain You Dry</u>, New York: McGraw-Hill, 2001.

Black, J. and G. Enns <u>Better Boundaries: Owning and Treasuring Your Own Life</u>, Oakland, CA: New Harbinger, 1997.

Clarken, John, Frank Yeomans and Otto Kernberg, <u>Transference-focused Psychotherapy. Psychotherapy for Borderline Personality</u>, NY: Wiley, 1998.

Cozolino, L., <u>The Neuroscience of Human Relationships: Attachment and the Developing Brain</u>. NY: Norton, 2006.

Crawford, TN, Cohen, First, MB, Skodol, AE, Kasen, S & Johnson, J.G. (2008) "Comorbid Axis I and Axis II disorders in early adolescence: Prognosis for 20 years later." <u>Archives of General Psychiatry</u>, 24, 389-393.

Dobbs, David "The Orchid Children" New Scientist, January 28, 2012, 42-45.

Eddy, Bill, <u>Don't Alienate the Kids</u>, San Diego, CA: HCI Press, 2010.

Eddy, Bill, <u>It's All Your Fault</u>, Santa Ana, CA: Janis Publications, 2008.

Huff, Tanya, <u>The Truth of Valor</u>, NY: DAW Books, 2010.

Managing High Conflict People In Court, San Diego, CA: HCI Press, 2008.

Fruzzetti, Alan and Marsha Linehan, The High Conflict Couple: A Dialectical Behavior Therapy Guide to Finding Peace, Intimacy and Validation, Oakland, CA: New Harbinger, 2006.

Gilcetti, and Nicki Crick Journal of Development and Psychopathology—mid-late 2009, 2 special issues on PD and childhood.

Kranowitz, Carol and Lucy Jane Miller, The Out-of-Sync Child: Recognizing and Coping with Sensory Processing Disorder, Rev. Ed., NY: Skylight Press, 2005.

Kapuchinski Stan Say Goodbye to Your PDI: Recognize People Who Make You Miserable and Eliminate Them from Your Life for Good, Deerfield Beach, FL: Health Communications, 2007.

Kreger, Randi and Paul Mason Stop Walking on Eggshells: Taking Your Life Back When Someone You Care About Has Borderline Personality Disorder, Oakland, CA: New Harbinger, 1998.

Kreger, Randi and James P. Shirley The Stop Walking On Eggshells Workbook, Oakland, CA: New Harbinger, 2002.

Linehan, Marsha M Skills Training Manual for Treating Borderline Personality Disorder, New York: Guilford Press, 1993.

Lund, John Lewis How to Hug A Porcupine: Dealing with Toxic and Difficult Personalities.: Educational Resources Associates, 1999.

Lyons-Ruth, Karlen, et. al. "Expanding the concept of unresolved mental states: hostile/helpless states of mind on the Adult Attachment Interview." Developmental Psychopathology, (2005) 17:1-23.

Maddock, James and Noel Larson, Incestous Families: An Ecological Approach to understanding and Treatment, NY: Norton, 1995.

Maddock, James and Noel Larson, "The Ecological Approach to Incestuous Families." In Handbook of Stress, Trauma and the Family. D. Catherall (Ed) NY: Brunner-Routledge, p. 367-393.

McWilliams, Nancy, Psychoanalytic Diagnosis, Second Edition: Understanding Personality Structure in the Clinical Process, NY: Guilford Press, 2011.

Ronson, Jon, The Psychopath Test: A Journey Through the Madness Industry. NY: Riverhead Books, 2011.

Miller, Aec, Jill Rathus and Masha Linehan <u>Dialectical Behavior Therapy with Suicidal Adolescents</u>, NY: Guilford Press, 2007.

National Association for Mental Illness (www.nami.org)

National Education Alliance for Borderline Personality Disorder (neabpd@aol.com), P.O. Box 974, Rye, NY 10580 (914) 835-9011.

O'Donohue, Wm., Katherine Fowler, Scott Lilienfied <u>Personality Disorders: Toward the DSM V</u>, Sage, 2007.

Paris, Joel <u>Borderline Personality Disorder: A Multidimensional Approach</u>, Washington, DC: Psychiatric Press, 1994.

Personality Disorders Awareness Network (www.pdan.org) 490 Sun Valley Drive, Suite 205, Roswell, GA 30076.

Wilson, ST, Stanley, B, Oquendo, MA, Brent, DA, Huang, YY, Mann, JJ (2008) "Tryptophan Hydroxylase A218C polymorphism is related to diagnosis, but not suicidal behavior, in borderline personality disorder". <u>American Journal Medical Genetics</u>, published on-line.

Wilson, ST, Stanley, B, Oquendo, MA, Brent, DA, Huang, YY, Mann, JJ (2008) <u>The Tryptophan Hydroxylase A218C Polymorphism Interacts with History of Childhood Abuse to Increase Risk for Borderline Personality Disorder</u>, submitted.

Simmons, Rachel, <u>Odd Girl Out: The Hidden Culture of Aggression in Girls</u>, NY: First Mariner Book, 2002.

Young, Jeffrey, Janet Klosko and Marjorie Weishaar <u>Schema Therapy: A Practitioner's Guide</u>, New York: Guilford, 2006.

"The longitudinal course of borderline psychopathology: 6-year prospective follow-up of the phenomenology of borderline personality disorder." <u>American Journal of Psychiatry</u>, (2003) 160: 274-283.

Zanarini, M., Reasons for Change in Borderline Personality Disorder (and Other Axis II Disorders) Psych Clinic North American, (2008) 31: 505-515.

Printed in Great Britain
by Amazon